Costa Rica

A Country Guide

Costa Rica
A Country Guide

Tom Barry

The Inter-Hemispheric Education Resource Center

Albuquerque, New Mexico

Published by the Inter-Hemispheric Education Resource Center

ISBN: 0-911213-36-8

Library of Congress Catalog Card Number: 89-81476

The Inter-Hemispheric Education Resource Center
Box 4506 * Albuquerque, New Mexico * 87196-4506

Acknowledgments

Costa Rica: A Country Guide is to a great extent a collective product of the Resource Center staff. Diligent research assistance came from Jenny Beatty, Joan MacLean, Felipe Montoya, Debra Preusch, and Thomas Weiss. In addition, Jenny Beatty guided the book from the manuscript page to the typeset book with her wordprocessing skills, while Debra Preusch, in addition to interviewing and research assistance, organized and oversaw the various stages of the making of this book—from making travel arrangements to dealing with the printer. Chuck Hosking edited the manuscript, and LaDonna Kutz proofread the book.

I would also like to thank friends and associates in Costa Rica, including Iliana Matamoros, Diego Low, and Jean Patterson for their hospitality; Linda Holland for the use of office and phone; Carlos Sojo for a variety of research assistance and for sharing his insights about Costa Rican politics and economy; and Lezak Shallat for all her suggestions and assistance, including commenting on the manuscript. Martha Honey and Marc Edelman also provided valuable comments on the manuscript, suggesting ways to improve the book's clarity and analysis.

Table of Contents

Introduction   **1**

Politics   **7**
Government   7
   The Reforms and Revolt in the Forties   7
   The State Under Attack   9
   Structure of Government   10
   Drugs and Corruption   11
Political Parties and Elections   11
   National Liberation Party   13
   Social Christian Unity Party   15
   The Left and Regional Parties   16
   The Right   18
Foreign Policy   18
Peace Process   19
Human Rights   21

Military   **23**
Security Forces   23
Paramilitary Groups   24

Economy   **27**
The State of the Economy   27
   Privatization of the State   29
   Back to Export Model   31
   Problems That Will Not Go Away   32
Agriculture   34
   The Rise of Precarismo   36

The Dessert Economy: Coffee, Bananas, Sugar   37
Industry and Finance   39
    Privatization of the Finance Industry   40

Society and Environment   41
Popular Organizing   41
Labor and Unions   45
    Obstacles Facing Labor Unions   48
    Solidarismo Takes Off   49
Schools and Students   52
Media   54
Health   59
Religion   61
    Rise of Evangelical Movement   63
Nongovernmental Organizations   65
Women and Feminism   67
Native People   69
Refugees   71
Environment   72

Foreign Influence   77
U.S. Foreign Policy   77
U.S. Trade and Investment   79
U.S. Economic Aid   82
    Assisting the Private Sector   83
    Uncertain Future   87
U.S. Military Aid   88
Other Foreign Interests   89
    Ties with Taiwan   90

Reference Notes   93

Appendices
Statistics   97
Chronology   99
Bibliography   105
For More Information   107

The Resource Center

The Inter-Hemispheric Education Resource Center is a private non-profit research and policy institute located in Albuquerque, New Mexico. Founded in 1979, the Resource Center produces books, policy reports, and other research about U.S. foreign relations with third world countries. Among its most popular materials are *The Central America Fact Book* and the quarterly *Bulletin* mailed to subscribers for $5 annually ($7.50 outside the United States). For a catalogue of publications, please write to the Resource Center, Box 4506, Albuquerque, NM 87196.

Costa Rica

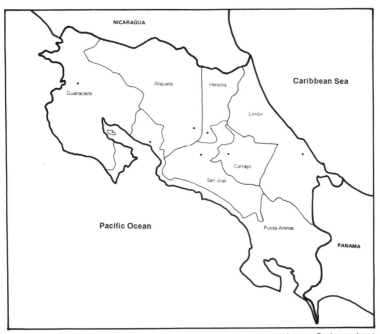

Inforpress Centroamericana

Introduction

Costa Rica is different, and Costa Ricans are proud of it. Statistical indicators of literacy and living conditions explain only part of this difference. It is the other, unquantified qualities that set the *ticos* (common term for Costa Ricans) and their beautiful country apart: taxi cab drivers telling you to fasten your seat belt, warnings about smoking in public places, the diversity of cultural offerings, police stopping to help you change a tire, respect for lines, and a multitude of parks and recreation areas.

Impossible to miss is the extreme pro-U.S. undercurrent in Costa Rican society. Three-time president José "Pepe" Figueres, an avid admirer of the American Way (although also a frequent critic of U.S. foreign policy in Central America), contributed to this fondness for all things "gringo." It also arises from Costa Rica's own feeling of isolation from Latin America.

In many ways, Costa Rica resembles an industrialized nation. Consumerism is a cultural phenomenon; and despite the atmosphere of freedom, there is a conformism, passivity, and relative absence of analytical thinking that reminds one of the United States. A strong democratic tradition and respect for human rights distinguishes Costa Rica from other countries in its turbulent region, but there is also a marked lack of independent community organization and political participation outside of the electoral process.

Costa Ricans, especially those of the central mesa, are more retiring than *ticos* on the coasts, where one finds much less introversion and less "proper" language. Throughout the country there exists a degree of order and respect for privacy and law that one seldom sees elsewhere in Central America.

A largely mountainous area, where cross-isthmus travel is difficult except on the few main highways, Costa Rica is a small country, not quite as large as West Virginia. It is among the most homogeneous societies in the world. Ninety-seven percent of Costa Ricans are of either European or *mestizo* stock, with little real distinction between the two.

Some 2 percent of Costa Ricans are of African-Caribbean descent. These black residents live mostly on the Atlantic coast around the port town of Limón. Brought from the West Indies to build railroads and work on the banana plantations of United Fruit, black Costa Ricans were largely confined to the Atlantic coast region until the late 1940s when changes in the country's constitution and travel regulations removed their second-class status. Intermarriage and easier access from San José are among the reasons that the Atlantic coast is gradually losing its Caribbean flavor. The Limón department, although the location of the country's main port, is among the poorest and most neglected in Costa Rica. In 1989 the Permanent Council for the Study and Solution of the Problems of Limón (CPESPL) led a department-wide general strike to demand the government respond to requests for increased wages and public services. Costa Rica never had a large native population — one reason why Costa Ricans are generally lighter-skinned than other Central Americans. Today, less than 0.5 percent of the society is Indian.

Costa Rica has achieved a 93 percent literacy rate. Higher education is of exceptional quality, but many *ticos* are emigrating because of better-paying opportunities in the United States and other industrialized countries. Yet another distinction of Costa Rica, a country of 2.9 million inhabitants, is its relatively low population growth (2.7 percent compared with 3 percent or higher in the rest of the region).

Costa Ricans are proud of themselves and their nation, and rightly so. Yet this pride is often tinged with racism and an alienating elitism. Despite its many attributes, Costa Rica is not the paradise that government tourist brochures describe. While the national park system is well advanced, rapid deforestation may mean the country will be importing wood by the end of the century. Hunger and poverty are not the powder kegs of its northern neighbors on the isthmus, but one-tenth of Costa Ricans live in absolute poverty. Malnutrition is increasing, as is obesity. Over one-third of adult women and one-fifth of adult men are dangerously overweight.

Corner bars are almost as common in Costa Rica as the corner *pulpería* (general store). An estimated 17 percent of adult Costa Ricans have drinking problems. Crime is rampant, as the many homes with barred windows and doors (even in the countryside) amply testify. As neoliberal economic principles and neoconservative political thinking have set the tone for political discourse in recent years, so have individualism and a search for easy money come to characterize many social and economic relations.

In Costa Rica, the government has traditionally taken itself seriously as a mediator between classes, and the resulting reforms have created the most egalitarian society in the region. Guarantees of education, pensions, and free health care represent opportunities rare elsewhere in Central America. Yet serious inequities in income and land distribution do exist, and are getting worse. In the mid-1980s the top 10 percent of the society received 37 percent of the wealth while the bottom 10 percent was left with 1.5 percent.[1] The absence of serious land reform has created a large landless peasant population in a countryside with vast tracts of uncultivated land often owned by foreigners or rich city dwellers who like to retire to their ranches for a country weekend.

Costa Rica is a land of legends and myths. It is known as the land of the yeoman farmer, but history only partially affirms this vision of the past. While an historic labor shortage and the territory's distance from the colony's center in Guatemala did give rise to a more democratic division of land and labor, an agroexport oligarchy and merchant elite dominated the country's economy and politics. Thirty-three of the 44 men who served as president of the country between 1821 and 1970 were descendants of three original colonizers.[2]

Another myth that marks Costa Rica is that it is a land of peace. While there is much to support this self-concept, the commitment to peace oftentimes seems more like a public-relations ploy than a shared political vision. The rise of rightwing paramilitary groups that count on government support, the increasingly violent response to popular organizing, the visible rise in militarization, and the country's warm relations with such countries as Taiwan, Israel, El Salvador, and the United States all tarnish the myth of peace that Costa Rica currently uses to promote foreign tourism and investment.

In 1981 Costa Rica achieved a less enviable distinction. An economic crisis put this touted paradise on the international financial map for being the first underdeveloped country to suspend debt payments. While the worst of the crisis has passed, its consequences have already begun to reshape the nation. The commitment to broad social welfare within the limits of capitalism that was a national feature since the 1940s began to weaken in the 1980s under international pressure for debt payments and financial restructuring. As a result, large holes began appearing in the safety net carefully woven over three decades of government programs.

From 1982 to 1990 the U.S. Agency for International Development (AID) pumped over $1.3 billion in economic aid into Costa Rica. Supplemented by large loans from the World Bank and the International Monetary Fund (IMF), this injection of foreign capital has permitted

Costa Rica to survive its economic crisis. The foreign largesse which brought Costa Rica from the brink of collapse to a new period of economic growth has political foundations. The generosity of the United States and the multilateral banks can be at least partially explained by their interest in maintaining Costa Rica as a showcase of democracy and dependent capitalist development in this region where traditional political structures are crumbling.

But foreign aid and economic recovery have come with a price: the imposition of harsh austerity measures, a restructuring of financial priorities, and a revamped development model. The "reforms" being imposed in the structural-adjustment process run contrary to the economic model of public sector-led modernization that has characterized Costa Rica since the early 1940s. A centerpiece of this modernization—the nationalized banking system—is being undermined, and once again the agroexport sector occupies a privileged place in the nation's economic priorities. Also under attack is the country's social-service infrastructure, as ministry budgets are being trimmed and many public-sector institutions are under foreign pressure to privatize.

The resulting conservative adjustment of the Costa Rican economy has attracted new private investors, primarily foreign, who also insist on certain conditions for their financial commitment. In the face of this increasing control by international financial institutions and the new wave of control by foreign investors, Costa Rican economist Leonardo Garnier observed, "Without national sovereignty, it makes little sense to talk of democracy."[3]

The country has opened its doors to U.S. investors, land speculators, tourists, and even fugitives from the law. Anything with a U.S. label is valued in Costa Rica. The country has two American Legion posts, and an American Realty Company that specializes in selling Costa Rican real estate to foreigners. There are limits, though. One U.S. citizen, John Hull, was finally indicted in 1989 by a Costa Rican court after the Iran-Contra hearings revealed what many already knew about the rancher's drug-trafficking and arms-running operations with the contras.

All of this is changing the ethos of Costa Rica. It is not happening overnight, but Costa Rica is becoming visibly more stratified and divided. Without money available to buy land to appease the landless, the government is responding to rural unrest with repression. Faced with the prospects of unemployment or low-paying jobs, sectors of the urban poor are responding with crime. Where negotiations and concessions once characterized the society, confrontations are becoming endemic.

While it is clearly the international financial institutions in tandem with their local allies in business and government that are directing the restructuring, they are not alone. Throughout the society there is a rightwing populism that has allowed the process to proceed without widespread public dissent. The domination of political thought in Costa Rica by two political parties and the rightist media contribute to a superficial understanding of the severity of the changes underway.

After two successive administrations by the National Liberation Party (PLN), the 1990s opened to the election of Rafael Angel Calderón of Social Christian Unity Party (PUSC). The PLN had pulled the country out of the 1979-1982 economic crisis, but socioeconomic conditions were visibly deteriorating by the late 1980s. Campaigning on a populist platform that downplayed his party's economic conservatism, Calderón won the election. Costa Rican voters were ready for a change, but President Calderón proved to be deeply committed to a neoliberal philosophy that stressed free trade, export promotion, dominance of the private-sector, and a scaled-back public sector.

Under the Calderón government, Costa Rica entered the General Agreement on Tariffs and Trade (GATT) and signed free-trade accords with Mexico and the United States. Plans to reduce the government's food allotments to the poor, lay off more than 7,000 public employees, and increase utility rates gained the government the good graces of the World Bank, International Monetary Fund, and the U.S. Agency for International Development. Although direct economic aid from Washington decreased, the government's economic policies opened the doors to increased multilateral funding as well as an infusion of aid from Japan.

The conservative structural-adjustment program initiated by the PLN was being even more vigorously pursued by the Calderón government. As a result, the social and economic character of Costa Rica was rapidly changing. Instead of promoting local food production and manufacturing for the local or regional market, the government pushed tourism and export-oriented production of vegetables, flowers, and garments. The social contract that once existed between the government and the country's workers and peasants has been largely discarded in the interests of cutting the fiscal deficit and tending to the interests of the private sector and international lending agencies.

During the late 1980s structural adjustment resulted in increased exports and a smaller budget deficit. It seemed that economic stability had been achieved, prompting President Arias to proclaim that Costa Rica would soon be entering the ranks of the developed nations. By the end of Calderón's first year, however, the country seemed to be entering a new period of economic crisis. Most serious was a widening trade deficit. The country had thrown its doors open to the international economy and was paying the price. A recession in the United States and an increasingly competitive world market for agricultural exports translated into reduced export earnings for Costa Rica. At the same time, the country was having to find dollars to pay for increased imports. Reacting to the rise in grain imports, farmers called for a policy of "food sovereignty" while domestic manufacturers complained they could not compete with cheaper foreign goods.

Per capita economic growth declined from 2.8 percent in 1989 to 1 percent in 1990--a sign of a decelerating economy. Higher than predicted inflation rates have depressed consumer spending and kept wage rates below the increased cost-of-living. Although reduced, a persistent budget deficit also threatened the country's economic stability. While the electricity and telephone rates soared, the government proved decidedly reluctant to tax the wealthy to raise needed revenues. Economists are concerned that further efforts to stabilize the economy through tighter credit and a stepped-up pace of currency devaluation could push the economy into a deep recession.

Most disturbing is the steady increase in poverty. According to government reports, 30 percent of Costa Ricans now live in poverty, while the United Nations estimates that at least 40 percent of the population are now poverty-stricken. To make ends meet amid rising unemployment and inflation, Costa Ricans are moving into the informal sector. Twenty-five percent of the country's workers now labor as street vendors or in other informal jobs--up from 9 percent in 1980.

The country's labor and farmer movements felt defrauded by President Calderón, who had promised an extensive social program during his electoral campaign. Instead, they found themselves increasingly left out of all government planning. Demands by labor unions for cost-of-living increases have, for example, been ignored in favor of restrictive wage policies advocated by the private sector.

A year after Calderón took office a new wave of social discontent began to take hold in Costa Rica. But neither the opposition parties nor the various popular organizations seemed capable of formulating an alternative political economic vision for Costa Rica. Unless public protests increase dramatically and a progressive political opposition develops, it is likely that during the remainder of the Calderón administration the neoliberal reforms set in place in the 1980s will continue--thereby further separating the country from its social-democratic past.

Chapter 1

Politics

Government

Government in Costa Rica is distinguished by its pervasive presence. The degree to which the public sector has assumed responsibility for social welfare (in terms of education, health, and social-assistance programs) is comparable to a similar commitment by many European states. The Costa Rican government is also economically active, having extended public-sector control to such areas as banking, petroleum refining, and utilities. Because of this broad participation in society and the economy, the Costa Rica public sector has been labeled variously as a benefactor state, welfare state, interventionist state, and even as a state capitalist or socialist state.

Since the early 1980s the Costa Rican state has been under attack from within and without. Leading the offensive have been the World Bank, International Monetary Fund (IMF), and the U.S. Agency for International Development (AID)—institutions which have found willing, even enthusiastic allies within the country's business and political community. Excessive public-sector spending and state intervention in the economy have been blamed for most of the country's economic ills.

The Reforms and Revolt in the Forties

Big government in Costa Rica began in the 1940s as part of the social reforms initiated by the Social Christian government of Rafael Angel Calderón Guardia. Such reforms as the institution of a labor code, a system of social security, and social-assistance programs were an attempt to modernize Costa Rican society. In its attempt to push through these controversial reforms, the Social Christian government counted on the backing of both the Catholic church under Archbishop Víctor Sanabria and the communist Popular Vanguard Party (PVP).

In 1948 another unlikely coalition overthrew the *calderonistas* after complaints of a fraudulent election in which conservatives were denied the presidency. The conservatives and Social Democrats, led by José Figueres, teamed up to seize state power in what is fondly remembered by some as the "Revolution of 1948." In the 18 months that followed, Figueres put a social-democratic imprint on Costa Rican government that has endured for four decades. The social reforms of the *calderonistas* were preserved and extended while new measures, such as the nationalization of banking and the abolition of the army, established the revolutionary thrust of the Figueres leadership. The social-democratic character of the new Costa Rican state was further insured by the progressive nature of the Constitution of 1949. As agreed, Figueres ceded power in 1949 to the conservatives, led by candidate Otilio Ulate Blanco. Four years later, Figueres won the presidency as leader of the newly constituted National Liberation Party (PLN).

For three decades, until the late 1970s, government expanded, with public-sector investment and spending occupying an ever larger role in the national economy. Within Costa Rica the steady growth of the state met with widespread approval. For the social democrats, it was the necessary result of their development philosophy and anti-oligarchic convictions. For industrialists and the modernizing bourgeoisie, the public sector had been, for the most part, a partner in economic advances in Costa Rica for over 30 years. And for state technocrats, bureaucrats, and the large public-sector workforce, the benefactor state provided economic security. The state itself set in place an infrastructure of housing, education, and health services that the lower and middle classes came to depend on.

State intervention in the economic sector expanded and evolved in the post-civil war years. The bank nationalization of 1949 established the class character of state interventionism, which succeeded in breaking the traditional economic hold of the agroexport oligarchy while promoting new economic interests, including those of an emerging industrial sector and a rising middle class. Subsidized credit was made available to these dynamic new interests, and the public sector set in place an economic and social infrastructure to accommodate their growth.

In the 1960s government moved (with some ambivalence) to facilitate the national economy's participation in the Central America Common Market by providing industrialists with protective tariffs and by opening up the country to U.S. transnationals. The Costa Rican state became not only a promoter of economic modernization but also a participant. Various corporations were nationalized in the public interest, and in the

1970s government began to promote economic growth by venture capital investment through a new public corporation called Costa Rica Development Corporation (CODESA).[1]

The other side of state interventionism was the state as a popular benefactor. An expansive bureaucracy was created to meet the education, health, and other basic needs of society. This commitment to the general welfare of the populace stemmed in part from the Social Christian and social-democratic ideals held by the country's modernizing ruling class since the 1940s. It was also a reaction to demands by a strong union movement in the 1940s for an increased share of national wealth. In the decades since the 1948 civil war, government social services have been maintained and extended as a conscious attempt to preserve social peace.

The government never encouraged independent organizing by the working class or peasants, and in numerous cases repressed such movements. But rarely has it ignored popular demands. In the interests of pacifying class conflict, the state has often responded with new social programs and new state agencies. In the 1960s its reaction to the problem of increasing landlessness was the creation of the Lands and Colonization Institute. In the 1980s it responded to militant demands for low-income housing with the promise to build 80,000 new homes. In this way, the government has maintained social peace and eased class conflict while reinforcing its own legitimacy. Referring to the capacity of the Costa Rican state to absorb class conflict, Chilean sociologist Diego Palma observed: "The key to Costa Rica is the political ability of its dominant class to impose a system that corresponds to that group's interests, and to have society as a whole accept this system as legitimate." This success is built on the recognition of the political and economic elite that the maintenance of social peace requires some compromise.[2]

The State Under Attack

In the late 1970s the Costa Rican development model began to crack due to widening trade imbalances and budget deficits and deepening balance-of-payments problems. The state was no longer able to pay its bills — opening the way for a conservative free-market or neoliberal attack on the entire social-democratic model. The main instruments of this assault on the public sector were the privatization of public-sector institutions, an austerity budget that trimmed social services, and the discontinuation of government subsidies, guarantees, and protections to small farmers.

It is unlikely that neoliberal remedies will ever be fully implemented, given the degree to which such reforms as nationalized banking, social security, public health, and public education have been integrated into Costa Rican society. Nonetheless, a steady but gradual paring away of the reformist state is underway in Costa Rica. By the year 2000 only skin and bones may remain of the protections and services offered by government at the beginning of the 1980s.

For three decades the Costa Rican state developed a certain social contract that, in exchange for social reforms and small favors, guaranteed a relatively passive popular movement. But more than social reforms, the public sector led the way for the transformation and modernization of the productive sector and the modification of the economy's distributive mechanism. Through the intervention of the state, the evolution of Costa Rican society took a direction that was not entirely dictated by market economics. It was the same direction taken by many industrial states, and for many years gave the country an economic and political stability that was the envy of the underdeveloped world.[3] Finally, however, the country's narrow economic base was no longer able to sustain the development model to which it had so long aspired.

Structure of Government

The actual governing of Costa Rica is managed by a national government divided into three branches — executive, legislative, and judicial — with the executive branch exercising disproportionate control. Nonetheless, the Legislative Assembly is well developed and limits presidential power somewhat more than in other Latin American nations, although there still has been a history of excessive rule by decree. Lately, the Legislative Assembly has asserted more authority, for example, over the approval of foreign-aid agreements, out of concern that these package agreements often infringe on national sovereignty. The 1949 Constitution, amended in 1969, limits the president and the deputies of the 57-member unicameral Legislative Assembly to four-year, non-successive terms.

After two successive National Liberation Party (PLN) administrations, the government passed into the hands of the rival Social Christian Unity Party (PUSC) in May 1990. Rafael Calderón Fournier succeeded President Oscar Arias after a narrow election victory in February 1990 in which he received 52 percent of the vote. The elections also gave the PUSC control of the legislature — 29 seats for the PUSC against 25 for the outgoing PLN and three for smaller parties. This will be the first time since 1953 that the PLN has been relegated to minority status in the legislature. (After 1978 it was also a minority but joined a majority coalition with other minority members.)

Drugs and Corruption

The integrity of politics and government in Costa Rica are increasingly being tainted by revelations of high-level corruption, influence-peddling, and association with drug trafficking. The openness of Costa Rican society and the attractiveness of the country itself have long made it a favorite place of exile for international crooks and villains. Their names range from U.S. financier Robert Vesco to Mexican drug figure Caro Quintero and Hosjabar Yazdani, the former executioner for the Shah of Iran. The 1989 flight from Costa Rica of rancher and prominent contra supporter John Hull, who was accused of drug trafficking and gun running, also sullied the reputation of Costa Rica. The international rogues who find a home in Costa Rica often count on favors from members of the political elite. In the late 1980s this high-level corruption came under the glare of international attention when high government officials and party officials were linked with reputed drug traffickers. A close associate of President Arias was arrested for laundering drug money, and it was revealed in the U.S. Congress that both of the country's leading political parties had accepted large campaign contributions from the Noriega regime of Panama.

The contras and the CIA-created network that supported them left behind a legacy of drug-smuggling and gun-running, while at the same time contributing to the increasing militarization of the country's police forces. A 1990 report by the U.S. Drug Enforcement Administration (DEA) estimated that at least a ton of cocaine passes through the country each month, while a thousand tons of marijuana are produced annually in Costa Rica. Following the U.S. invasion of Panama, Costa Rica became a favored spot for drug traffickers to launder money.

Political Parties and Elections

In Costa Rica elections are an honored tradition of which citizens are rightly proud. Election politics have found a place in the country's culture, with the whole society joining in the fiesta of flag-waving, car parades, and political debate. The candidates from the country's two leading political parties — National Liberation Party (PLN) and the Social Christian Unity Party (PUSC) — always stand at center stage during this national celebration and affirmation of Costa Rican democracy. The two parties have alternately held power over the last three decades. Participation in elections has remained high in contrast to rising abstentionism in other

Central American countries. The 8.2 percent abstentionism in 1990 was similar to previous presidential elections.

Modern political history in Costa Rica begins in 1948, the year that José Figueres led a "revolution" to contest a fraudulent election and the expanding influence of the Popular Vanguard Party (PVP). The government led by Figueres and PLN was not a break with the past but an expansion and deepening of the social reforms initiated by Calderón. At the same time, though, the coup led by Figueres brought with it widespread violations of civil liberties against the leftist supporters of Calderón and was regarded by many as narrowing of the democratic opening. The nationalization of the banking system and the strengthening of social security exemplified the "statist" and benefactor nature of the 1948 "revolution." From the beginning, the PLN promoted an anticommunist populism that was tempered by anti-oligarchic reforms and social-democratic developmentalism. In the 1980s, however, the PLN's economic policies veered sharply to the right.

Political democracy, characterized by regular elections and a tradition of social compromise, is deeply ingrained in Costa Rican society. Still, there is a superficial quality about Costa Rican democracy that might eventually undermine its stability. Many Costa Ricans vote out of family tradition for the *calderonistas* or the *figueristas*, not out of any ideological conviction. In many ways, elections represent the outer limits of the democratic process in Costa Rica. Once the party flag-waving and actual voting are over, Costa Rican citizens tend to withdraw from the political arena, leaving professional politicians to manage the affairs of the nation.

Even during the election campaigns, democracy and popular participation in Costa Rica has an increasingly superficial quality. Sloganeering and personality politics have replaced serious debate. And as if Costa Rican politics were not already enough like national politics in the United States, both parties have taken to hiring top U.S. election consultants to guide their campaigning. Rafael Calderón Fournier, son of PUSC's mentor, has hired Roger Ailes, who produced the hard-hitting campaign commercials for George Bush, while the PLN brought on political consultant Joel McCleary, who has worked with U.S. Democratic Party candidates. Not unlike the United States, politics is rapidly deteriorating into a contest of television images rather than a forum for debate about national priorities.

While the education system has created a literate nation, there is an alarming intellectual conformity and lack of tolerance for ideological diversity in Costa Rican society. A rightwing media is largely responsible for the deepening conservatism. Indeed, it is the media that set the bounds of acceptable political discourse. Also eating away at the honorable traditions of Costa Rica-style democracy is the propagation by the media, business elite, and AID of a neoconservative philosophy embodied in the slogan, "Private Enterprise Produces Liberty."

More than four decades have passed since 1948, and there is little doubt that serious changes are called for if the country is to face adequately the economic and political challenges of the future. The success of the 1948 "revolution" came from its ability not only to deal with short-term problems but also to create a system of governing and social relations that anticipated future challenges. In the 1980s all the political parties, including the leftist parties, looked to the right for solutions to the crisis. It remains to be seen if the private-sector solutions being proposed and implemented will ensure the political and economic stability that all Costa Ricans desire.

National Liberation Party

Until his June 1990 death "Don Pepe" Figueres, who led the 1948 "revolution" against the *calderonistas*, served as the patriarch of the National Liberation Party (PLN) and was thrice president of Costa Rica. The PLN is the party that presided over the institution of a reformist, benefactor state. For 34 years, Figueres and the PLN, alternating in power with the opposition party, promoted a modern capitalist democracy with a substantial welfare component. Since 1982, however, the PLN's commitment to social reforms and social services has been counterbalanced by a strong component of neoliberal economic principles.

The party's standard-bearers in recent years, Presidents Luis Alberto Monge and Oscar Arias, ushered in an era of structural reform and cutbacks in the public sector. It is difficult to characterize the PLN's politics because of the party's diverse elements, from uncompromising neoconservatives like former Central Bank president Eduardo Lizano to more moderate leaders who still adhere to the social vision of Figueres. As the ruling party, the PLN incorporates many individuals who were more technocrats and bureaucrats than politicians.

Officially, the PLN is a social-democratic party and a member of the Socialist International. But its social-democratic ideals were largely shunted aside since 1982 in favor of economic policies advocated by the IMF, World Bank, and AID. Stopping short of complete capitulation, the PLN did not entirely embrace or enforce neoliberal solutions, choosing instead to implement a more pragmatic than ideological policy of economic reforms. Nonetheless, the contradictions between the stated social-democratic principles of the party and its conservative practices became increasingly pronounced.

Recriminations and political in-fighting ruptured the PLN in the late 1980s, and reports linking the party to drug money severely undermined its reputation. The party's leadership and direction was also vehemently contested by the Liberationist Youth (JL), which advocates a return to the "real social democracy" of the PLN. There is also a left-of-center wing of the PLN which opposes further privatization and favors an agricultural policy of food security and assistance to small farmers.

After two terms Costa Rican voters turned the PLN out of office in the 1990 general elections. Presidential candidate Carlos Manuel Castillo, a respected economist and former government official, stressed his greater experience and capacity for the presidency while reminding voters that the PLN had led the country out of the economic crisis of the early 1980s. The PLN stressed its political moderation, its commitment to neutrality, and its history of nation-building. Taking the PLN campaign to the Costa Rican public, Castillo was handicapped by deteriorating socioeconomic conditions for the country's poor, a background of party factionalism, public identification of the party with corruption and narcotrafficking, and the lack of a distinct political platform. Many citizens, including some of the party faithful, became increasingly disenchanted with the PLN because it had effectively dropped its long commitment to social-democratic developmentalism. As a result, the gap between the party leaders and the party's popular base widened ominously during the 1980s. A superior campaign by the PUSC, Castillo's lack of charisma, and voter concern that the PLN was establishing itself as the state party also contributed to Calderón's victory.

The close election, however, did not give a clear electoral mandate to the PUSC. With 47.2 percent of the vote and 25 seats in the Legislative Assembly, the PLN could form a strong opposition if the party can overcome its internal differences. There are factions within the party who have opposed the conservative economic direction the party took during the 1980s, and the PLN also has been weakened by a split between those who supported Castillo and a smaller faction who supported the more social-democratic Rolando Araya for the presidential nomination. In addition to Araya and Castillo, by early 1991 two other candidates were in the running for the PLN nomination for the 1994 presidential contest: José María Figueres, the son of the party patriarch, and the popular Margarita Penón de Arias, wife of former president Oscar Arias.

Social Christian Unity Party

The Social Christian Unity Party (PUSC), led by Rafael Calderón Fournier, represents the bloc of political parties that alternated in power with the PLN for the past 40 years. Since 1977 the bloc has functioned as the PUSC, which is a coalition of four parties: the Republican Calderonista Party (PRC), led by Rafael Calderón Fournier; the Democratic Renovation Party (PRD); the Christian Democratic Party (PDC), led by Rafael Grillo Rivera; and the Popular Unity Party (PUP), led by Cristian Tattenbach Iglesias. The PUSC backed Rodrigo Carazo in a successful bid for the presidency in 1978 but lost two successive election contests in the 1980s.

Although as a whole more conservative than the PLN, the PUSC encompasses two political tendencies.[4] Historically this political bloc has incorporated the reformist tradition of the 1940s. But the ideological right and the private-sector elite have also found a home in the PUSC and have dominated its leadership and policymaking. During the 1980s Calderón and other PUSC leaders were aggressively anti-Sandinista and criticized the PLN's failure to fully implement conservative structural-adjustment measures. The PUSC, which represents the more conservative and traditional members of the business elite, calls for complete and rapid financial restructuring and the dismantling of the reformist state.

The PUSC is a member of the International Democrat Union (IDU), established in 1983 as a global association of conservative political parties, including the Republican Party in the United States. Both the PUSC and the IDU have benefited from U.S. government funding channeled through the quasi-private National Endowment for Democracy (NED). In Costa Rica, NED funds have gone to the Association for the Defense of Freedom and Democracy, a rightwing organization run by PUSC officials.

President Rafael Calderón Fournier is the son of ex-president Rafael Angel Calderón Guardia (1940-1944), who introduced the country's labor code and social-security system. The working class is viscerally pro-Calderón in memory of his father's alliance with organized labor against the conservatives. Calderón won the PUSC convention's nomination handily, demonstrating his firm control of the party.

A graduate of the University of Costa Rica Law School in 1972, Calderón has never practiced law but devoted himself to politics. He served in the legislature from 1974 to 1978, and was foreign minister from 1978 to 1980. He unsuccessfully ran for president in 1982 and then again in 1986, when he lost substantial support to Arias because of what has been described as his "war-mongering." Careful not to make the same mistake in the latest round, Calderón strongly endorsed regional peace initiatives and maintained his distance from the ultra-conservative sectors critical of Arias' peace efforts.

In the 1990 election, Calderón, 41, was the less qualified but more attractive presidential candidate. During the campaign he adopted a populist rhetoric that made him the candidate of change and hope for those frustrated with PLN corruption and the poor and working people adversely affected by the PLN's conservative economic policies. Proving to be a skilled politician who could change with the times, Calderón presented himself as the "candidate of the poor" and promised not to levy new taxes, to create mechanisms that allow workers to share in company profits, and to make the government's low-income housing program less costly to beneficiaries. The populist content of the Calderón campaign together with widespread dissatisfaction with the PLN made the difference in the close election.

The conservative political and economic principles espoused by Calderón's advisers and cabinet members contrasted sharply with his campaign promises of economic democratization and government assistance for those adversely affected by the economic policies of the PLN governments. Most of those appointed came directly from the business sector and were more ideologically conservative than those that accompanied President Arias. The president of the Central Bank is a prominent member of the National Association for Economic Promotion (ANFE), which has campaigned for wholescale economic liberalization. The finance, economy and industry, planning, and foreign trade ministries are all in the hands of prominent businessmen and economists. Another business leader was appointed to head the agriculture ministry, and the security minister is a former president of the Union of Private Enterprise Chambers.[5] The nepotism practiced by President Rodrigo Carazo (who appointed 25 relatives to his administration) has come back to government with Calderón, who has named 23 cousins and in-laws to fill government posts.

The United States and other foreign lenders were pleased with the new government's willingness to extend the neoliberal economic reforms and austerity measures initiated by the previous PLN administrations. But the populist program that won Calderón the election was given short shrift. Unless the economy dramatically improves, which seems unlikely, the economic measures instituted by the Calderón adminstration--higher sales taxes and utility rates, severe cutbacks in social services and the public-sector workforce, and increased attention to export promotion-- may cost the PUSC the elections in 1994.

The Left and Regional Parties

The bipartisan character of electoral politics was underlined by the 1990 national elections in which five small parties attracted only 1.3

percent of the presidential vote. Failure to win 1.5 percent of the national vote meant that several small parties lost their legal status and chance to receive government funding. The February 1990 elections were another strong blow to the organized left in Costa Rica. Sectarian splits, personality fights, loss of a base among labor (particularly the banana workers), and difficulty in distancing themselves from their dogmatic past have been among the factors undermining the ability of the leftist parties to establish a popular base.

Since 1931 the Popular Vanguard Party (PVP), which has operated as the country's communist party, has been in the forefront of the workers' struggles and the leftist movement in Costa Rica. During the 1980s, however, it was weakened by internal splits, its inability to formulate a popular political agenda, and disastrous strikes by associated unions against the two U.S. banana companies.

In 1986 the party fractured, giving rise to the Costa Rican People's Party (PPC). As the 1990 elections approached, the leftist parties attempted to increase their base by moving away from strict Marxist-Leninist interpretations and appealing to all those popular sectors dissatisfied with the country's conservative direction. The PVP and the PPC, presenting a common platform under the banner of People United, was able to gain a single seat in the National Assembly, from San José, while the two other parties, Progress Party and Revolutionary Party of Workers in Struggle, were barely able to mobilize their few party militants.

The success of two regional parties, the General Union Party (PUGEN) based in Pérez Zeledón in the south and the National Agrarian Party (PAN) based in Limón, in winning a deputy seat was seen as a sign of increasing voter interest in having candidates that respond to the needs of local communities rather than representatives of the two major parties. The emergence of the PAN in Limón was also indicative of the mounting unrest in this area severely affected by the government's agricultural policies in the 1980s.[6]

Because of the poor national showing of the smaller parties, they were unable to qualify for government funding, which only the two leading parties, PLN and PUSC, will receive. According to Rodrigo Gutiérrez, the legislator representing People United, the current electoral system and bipartisan nature of Costa Rican politics do not give sufficient opportunity to small parties. The absence of a second round in the national elections also undermines the influence of minor parties.

Foreign Policy

The foreign policy of Costa Rica has traditionally reflected the Cold War orientation of U.S. foreign policy, but the country has occasionally charted a certain degree of independence from Washington. Such was the case during the first three years of the Carazo administration (1978-1982). Carazo's support for the Sandinistas, attempts to fortify relations among third world nations, and opposition to IMF structural adjustment created strains between the United States and Costa Rica. The space opened for this independent foreign policy during the Carter administration disappeared with the advent of the Reagan White House.[7]

With Luis Alberto Monge as president, Costa Rica became the pliant ally that the Reagan administration needed for its campaign against Nicaragua. By the end of his administration, however, Monge was attempting to stave off U.S. pressure to directly and openly support U.S.-led military aggression against Nicaragua. As a defensive measure, President Monge mobilized popular support for the country's traditional "proclamation of neutrality."

Although President Arias shared Washington's virulent anti-socialist and anti-Sandinista convictions, he saw the futility and counterproductive nature of the contra campaign. He petitioned Washington to dismantle the contra infrastructure in Costa Rica and began working with congressional Democrats on an alternative foreign policy for the region. Tensions arose between Arias and the White House — with the former advocating a strategy of negotiation and democratization while the latter maintained its allegiance to the contras. Economic aid was trimmed, and Arias was repeatedly snubbed by President Reagan and then by Bush. President Arias, for example, was not invited to attend Bush's inauguration. The differences between the Arias administration and Bush were also clearly evident in the Costa Rican government's failure to applaud the U.S. invasion of Panama.

The tensions that occasionally arose between Costa Rica and Washington had diminished by mid-1990 as a result of declining U.S. foreign-policy interest in the region. The new government of Calderón, who purports to be a personal friend of President Bush, is likely to stay closely aligned with the United States in foreign-policy matters. But Costa Rica will no longer be able to count on generous U.S. economic assistance now that the Sandinistas are no longer in power in neighboring Nicaragua.[8]

Although more successful than other Central American countries, Costa Rica has failed to supplement decreased U.S. aid with infusions of

European assistance. The astounding political changes in Eastern Europe will make it yet more difficult for Costa Rica to attract Western European aid.

Peace Process

As a candidate, Oscar Arias had promised the Costa Rican people that he would uphold the country's neutrality and support regional peace efforts. The growing refugee problem and Nicaragua's World Court suit against Honduras and Costa Rica which was damaging Costa Rica's international reputation were among the factors that pushed President Arias to offer his peace plan. Although the regional peace accords were a product of all five countries, President Arias did play a special role in guiding the process along, standing up to the Reagan administration along the way. For these efforts, Arias was awarded the Nobel Peace Prize.

The Contadora peace process had failed due to strong U.S. opposition and its failure to win the approval of Central American countries, with the exception of Nicaragua. The opportune nature of the Arias peace proposal and the fact that the Esquipulas accords included some advantages for all sides allowed them to flourish. The simultaneity and the time table for the implementation of the peace accords also distinguished them from the failed Contadora initiatives.[9]

Within Costa Rica, the accords signed in Esquipulas found support among both the peace and leftist communities and progressive social democrats alike. The media and hidebound business community looked upon the peace accords skeptically and critically, feeling, like the Reagan administration, that the proposal was being used by the Sandinistas to deepen their hold on the Nicaraguan government. More progressive elements within the business community welcomed the peace agreements, however, reasoning that they would result in a more stable business climate in the region.

The Bush administration brought U.S. foreign policy closer in line with U.S. allies in the region. With the threat of a regional war diminished, attention was again focused on Nicaragua rather than on Central America as a region. Questions of regional peace were reduced to a judgment about democratization in Nicaragua.

Other than the benefits resulting from all the favorable international publicity, Costa Rica was hardly affected by the peace accords. A National Reconciliation Commission was established in line with the agreements, but it has had little influence or visibility.

Objections from the right wing stalled approval of a Central America Parliament — an embarrassing circumstance for a country supposedly in the vanguard of the search for regional peace and democracy. Groups like the Movement for a Free Costa Rica claimed that a regional parliament would give new standing and credibility to the Nicaraguan revolution while unnecessarily involving Costa Rica in the regional political and military crisis. Although most popular sectors support the peace accords, widespread opposition emerged in 1988 to the Arias government for devoting more attention to international problems than to increasingly acute internal economic problems, such as the agricultural crisis.

Commenting on the lack of support for the regional parliament in Costa Rica, sociologist Edelberto Torres Rivas said, "Opponents of the parliament are operating under the false premise that Costa Rica's economy can flourish outside the Central American context by placing its products on third markets in the developed world. Our studies show that without regional integration not even Costa Rica can count on a national future."[10]

President Calderón, who in the past adopted hard-line and militaristic positions, campaigned in 1989-1990 on a platform of peace. Despite his campaign promise to push through approval for the Central American Parliament, the proposal continued to languish in the Legislative Assembly and the nation's courts. Calderón will be hard put to achieve the kind of international recognition and respect won by President Arias. Within Costa Rica there is little interest in increasing the country's political or economic association with the other more troubled nations of the isthmus. Although the Calderón administration did act as an intermediary between the Salvadoran guerrillas and government, its main foreign policy focus shifted to the economic arena. One possible direction for regional talks is on the economic front, examining ways to increase regional economic cooperation and trade. Here too, however, Costa Rica has shown itself to be more interested in bilateral solutions to trade and debt problems. It was the first country to sign a bilateral free-trade accord with Mexico, and has also joined Washington's Enterprise for the Americas Initiative.

Human Rights

As might be expected, the human rights situation in Costa Rica compares favorably with other countries in the region. However, the military and economic crisis that has assaulted Central America since the end of the 1970s has taken its toll on Costa Rica's reputation for liberty and democracy. Human rights abuses, such as arbitrary detentions, physical abuse and torture by security forces, repression of dissent, and the intimidation of political activists, became more common in the 1980s.

The marked increase in human rights violations was to some degree an outgrowth of the role played by Costa Rica in regional politics. Its willingness to join the U.S.-sponsored war against Nicaragua resulted in the same cycle of repression seen in other countries, although less extreme. In return for economic aid, the government permitted the militarization of the country, both through its clandestine support for the southern front of the contras and by accepting increased U.S. military aid and training for its own internal security forces. Among the side effects of this weakening of its vaunted neutrality was the rise of rightwing vigilante organizations and a related witch-hunt atmosphere directed at popular organizations and dissidents. Also closely related to the government's participation in the U.S.-sponsored anti-Sandinista campaign was the emergence of increased drug-trafficking and associated corruption.

At the forefront of denouncing human rights abuses is the Costa Rican Human Rights Committee (CODEHU) which claims that nearly 40,000 people have been detained without charges since 1985. (Unlike elsewhere in Central America, those arrested without charges are usually released the same day.) Some of these have been part of mass roundups by the Crime Prevention Unit. One such roundup focused on the capital's gay population. Visitors, including Nobel Peace Prize recipient Adolfo Pérez Esquivel, have been arbitrarily detained at the international airport. According to a 1988 report by Pax Christi International, those targeted for arbitrary detention are mostly undocumented foreigners, persons traveling to Nicaragua or Cuba, homosexuals, human rights advocates, certain religious activists, and members of leftist parties.[11]

Torture, while not widespread, has become a concern for the first time. In one case, a 13-year-old boy was detained, tortured with electric shock and needles, and then later released after the police learned that he had been mistakenly arrested. CODEHU has also alerted public attention to the sorry state of prisoners' rights. In 1987 over 40 percent of all prisoners were being held while awaiting trial.[12] CODEHU contends that local media have blocked the dissemination of information about human rights abuses, even to the extent of refusing to print paid denunciations of such violations.

Refugees, especially, felt the burden of increased political tension and the repressive behavior of the country's security forces. Those without papers were arrested and detained for long periods without being charged. Other sectors that were hit hard by repression included squatter groups and banana workers. They were forcibly evicted, arrested, and sometimes beaten. Squatters have been victimized by the private security forces of large landowners, many of them U.S. citizens.

Uniformed members of the security forces, however, are responsible for most human rights violations. Unlike elsewhere in Central America, there are no death squads, although rightwing paramilitary organizations emerged during the 1980s. (See Paramilitary Groups) The police justify arbitrary detentions, violent repression of demonstrations and squatters movements, and other human rights violations as necessary to maintain order and protect national security. Although the Rural Guard has been charged with most human rights abuses, the most serious violations have been attributed to the police of the Office of Judicial Investigations (OIJ) and the Security and Intelligence Department (DIS). When asked about the large number of arbitrary detentions, the DIS director replied they were necessary "to intimidate those 'bad' Costa Ricans who have been sniffed out."

In the late 1980s, with the ascent of the Central America Peace Plan and international attention focused on President Arias, the human rights climate in Costa Rica improved noticeably. CODEHU noted that Costa Ricans could, for the first time, talk about human rights problems without being labeled "unpatriotic." Police roundups were suspended and arbitrary detentions by immigration authorities became less frequent. Nonetheless, CODEHU charges that the broadly defined human rights of Costa Ricans are being violated daily. Besides the deteriorating state of prisoner rights, the organization points to such continuing problems as: the lack of freedom of expression due to rightwing control of the media, the worsening economic situation for the poor, the government's failure to honor workers' collective-bargaining rights or to guarantee the basic needs of its citizens, and the repression of *campesino* and worker organizations, particularly in rural areas.

In 1990-1991 the rise in anti-narcotics activity by U.S. and Israeli trained police has resulted in an increase in serious human-rights violations by overly ambitious police units. According to human-rights spokesperson Sylvia Porras, the main human-rights problem continues to be the Costa Rican police, whose "psychological profile has changed as a result of military training." She said the country no longer has a civilian police force: "What we have is a hidden army."

Chapter 2

Military

Security Forces

Soon after the 1948 civil war José Figueres abolished the army, bringing himself lasting distinction and giving Costa Rica its reputation as the "Switzerland of Central America." The decision to abolish the army was not "immaculately conceived," as Phillip Berryman of the American Friends Service Committee noted. Rather it came at the end of a war fought against a political coalition that had introduced the country's first social reforms. Figueres, who later would adopt and broaden the reforms first instituted by the Calderón government, abolished the army to eliminate a potential threat to the victorious National Liberation movement that he led.

Four decades later Costa Rica still does not have an army, but it does count on a rapidly growing police force, much of which has received military training. During the 1980s the number of police in the country doubled. Not only did the actual number of police increase, but the new security forces were also created. At least nine different police agencies now exist. Under the supervision of the Ministry of Justice is the police force of the Office of Judicial Investigations (OIJ), while the Ministry of Public Security administers the Security and Intelligence Department (DIS), the Civil Guard (GC), the Metropolitan Police, Crime Prevention Unit (UPD), and the Office of Drug Control. The Ministry of Government controls the Rural Assistance Guard (GAR) and the immigration police, while traffic police answer to the Ministry of Transportation and Public Works. The most recently created forces are the Special Investigation Police (PIE), under the Ministry of Public Security, and the Immediate Action Unit (UAI), a SWAT-like team known for its Rambo style.

Unlike most other Central American countries, where police and military come under a central command structure, each government ministry in Costa Rica controls its own respective security force. This absence of a common command structure has hindered the security forces from asserting more influence in Costa Rican society, but at the same time the disparate nature of the security forces renders them less accountable to public management. A problem of continuity exists in the security forces due to the persistence of the patronage system. All except for the top officers in the main security forces are dismissed when a new political power takes over government.

While other government agencies are shrinking, the ministries with police forces have experienced steady budget increases. In addition to larger tax allocations, Costa Rican security forces are also bloated from international aid from such countries as the United States, South Korea, and Taiwan for externally initiated military training and supplies, counterterrorism assistance, and narcotics programs.

An estimated 85 percent of foreign aid comes from the United States, either through the Department of Defense (DOD), AID, State Department's Bureau of International Narcotics (IMN), or the Drug Enforcement Administration (DEA).[1] Most DOD assistance goes to the Civil Guard, which is the more professional of the two main security forces. The Rural Guard, in contrast, maintains less of a national presence, in part because its members are recruited locally for police stations near their homes. Lately, U.S. assistance has focused on drug enforcement, including the training of dozens of Costa Rican anti-narcotics agents by Green Berets from Ft. Bragg, North Carolina.

The increasing militarization of the country's police forces and rising human rights violations have raised public concern about the development of a "secret army" in Costa Rica. The institution in mid-1990 of a new military-type ranking system, which replaces the present titles of Officer with Police Colonel down through Police Sergeant, reinforced this concern about militarization.

Paramilitary Groups

For a country without an armed opposition, Costa Rica hosts a surprisingly large number of rightwing paramilitary groups. The country has no tradition of vigilante activities but in the 1980s saw the emergence of a half-dozen volunteer organizations that proclaim the necessity of protecting the national fatherland against leftist threats. These groups drew from a wave of reactionary populism and *antisandinismo* that swept the country.

The Free Costa Rica Movement (MCRL) is the oldest, most visible, and most influential of the paramilitary organizations. It operates as a rightwing civic group with an armed offshoot. Founded in 1961 to "thwart Cuban expansionism," MCRL experienced a rebirth in the 1980s. While to the right of most Costa Ricans, MCRL does enjoy close ties to the media and the traditional business and agricultural elite. Many MCRL members are officials of the country's security forces, but the group has also received supplies and other support from the U.S. embassy. When MCRL spearheaded a violent protest in 1986 against the Central America Peace March, its most active stormtroopers were members of the Costa Rica Taxi Drivers Union. A union director and member of the MCRL directorate admitted that the U.S. embassy slipped MCRL information discrediting the march. According to an article in *The Progressive*, MCRL maintains links with such international groups as Alpha 66, White Hand Death Squad (Guatemala), and the World Anti-Communist League (WACL).[2]

The North Huetar Democratic Association, based in the northern area of San Carlos department, was founded in 1983 as a contra-support group. One close observer of the right wing described it as a militia group directed by U.S. rancher John Hull. Adolfo Louzao, a Vietnam veteran who organized the group's military training, lists among its accomplishments the destruction of squatter settlements and the quashing of a strike. Closely resembling the North Huetar group is the North Chorotega Democratic Association, also active along Costa Rica's politically sensitive border with Nicaragua.

Another vigilante group is Patria y Libertad (Country and Liberty), which took responsibility for the 1985 bombing of an electrical tower that was part of a grid which transferred power to Nicaragua. The action, which included mining the area around the tower, seriously discredited the organization and, by extension, other similar groups. Patria y Libertad includes former Somoza supporters and adherents of the Autonomous Guanacaste Movement, which calls for the secession and eventual statehood of Guanacaste department. Yet another rightwing paramilitary group is the Patriotic Union, which formed to defend the country against a possible Nicaragua invasion. One of its founders is Ludwig Starke, who allowed the U.S. government to train Cuban exiles on his ranch in preparation for the Bay of Pigs invasion in 1961.

As a percentage of the total population, the paramilitary groups represent only the shadowy fringe of Costa Rican society, but these groups enjoy close ties within government and business. The Monge administration provided critical support and legal cover for the paramilitary movement, and senior government officials, including the Minister of Security, were members. While the Arias administration officially distanced itself from the MCRL, one member noted that six of his cohorts held high positions in the Arias government. As in other Central American countries, the paramilitary movement overlaps to a large degree with the official security forces. Most groups are integrated into the National Reserve, and many of their members are also officers in the police forces.

The paramilitary movement also receives U.S. support. As members of government security groups, many have received training from U.S. Special Forces, and former Minister of Security Juan José Echeverria revealed that the CIA has unofficially supported the paramilitary forces as well.[3]

Chapter 3

Economy

The State of the Economy

Costa Rica's development bubble burst in 1980, when it suddenly found that it was technically bankrupt and in the midst of the worst recession in its history. The crisis was brought on by the rising interest rates the country found itself paying on its external debt – then the highest per capita debt in Latin America, most of which was owed to private U.S. banks. The context for the financial crisis, however, was the country's development model: an agroexport economy dependent on a few traditional crops, a protected industrial and import-dependent sector, and a benefactor state based on borrowed money. Rising oil prices and increasingly unfavorable terms of trade brought Costa Rica to the brink of collapse.

As one of the world's least impoverished third world countries, Costa Rica was not a favored recipient of foreign-development aid from institutions like the U.S. Agency for International Development (AID) and the World Bank. Neither had it received the emergency attention of the International Monetary Fund (IMF). Suddenly, Costa Rica became the focus of international financial concern. For one thing, foreign donors wanted to avoid the precedent of a third world country stopping interest payments on its debt – which Costa Rica did temporarily in 1981. Another concern, purely political, was the importance to the capitalist world, particularly the United States, that this southern neighbor of revolutionary Nicaragua maintain its economic and political stability. It was deemed essential to keep in good working form this prime example of capitalist democracy in Central America.

The 1980s, then, were a period when the financial and development remedies – commonly called structural adjustments – fostered by the U.S. government and the international financial institutions were tested. They included austerity measures that trimmed the government's social-services budget, the privatization of public-sector institutions, promotion of exports, and the economic liberalization (meaning the end of subsidies and protective pricing and tariffs) of trade and production.

By the mid-1980s Costa Rica had managed to shake the crisis. Its debt payments were back on track, its exports increased, and it had again achieved positive economic growth. It remains to be seen, however, whether this stability is a temporary result of large injections of foreign capital or whether it is a more long-lasting base for future economic growth and development. Also in doubt is whether a development model that successfully spurs economic growth necessarily improves socioeconomic conditions or might actually exacerbate inequitable patterns of income and resource distribution.

While many economic indicators pointed to a stabilized and even dynamic economy, two of the factors that precipitated the economic crisis in the early 1980s remain, namely an unshakable trade deficit and a high per capita foreign debt. International aid from the World Bank, AID, and the IMF have, for the time being, solved the earlier balance-of-payments crisis. While helping to restructure the Costa Rican economy, this aid has also played a major role in the restructuring of Costa Rican society. In the 1980s income and resources in Costa Rican society have become more concentrated. The tax system has, for example, become increasingly regressive, relying heavily on indirect taxes (like sales tax) rather than on direct taxes on income and property. Real wages have not reflected recent gains in national economic growth, and the social services originally designed to broaden the distribution of national income are being cut. A system of mini-devaluations at three-week intervals which depreciates the currency about 20 percent annually also disproportionately impacts on the buying power of the poor.

Writing in 1983, Costa Rican economist Juan Manuel Villasuso Etomba warned that the "acceleration of the process of concentration of income and wealth" would eventually undermine the traditional social peace in Costa Rica. Furthermore, the neoliberal policies adopted to address the crisis will reinforce these trends. According to Villasuso:

> The effect on the social, economic, and political structure of Costa Rica in the next few years and through to the end of the century is difficult to predict. But an enormous danger exists that in the not so distant future, the distribution system will no longer be "socially acceptable." At that time, Costa Rica's social harmony, which for decades has been an example for Central America and the world, may be brought into question.[1]

In his campaign, Calderón successfully sought the votes of those who felt victimized by the conservative economic policies of the PLN administrations. It is unlikely, however, that the populist message of his campaign will be translated into government policy. The first order of business of the new government was to lower the budget deficit and seek new accords with the IMF and the World Bank.

Particularly when compared with the state of the economy in the early 1980s, the economy seemed to be in good shape when the PLN handed over power to the PUSC. The country had experienced 5 percent growth in gross domestic income, inflation was down to 9 percent, and unemployment stood at 4 percent. When taking over the reins of government, the new administration was confronted by other, less auspicious statistics. During the last year of PLN rule the budget deficit had dangerously widened — projected to rise to at least $250 million by the end of 1990. Economic aid from Washington was down about $30 million, and an expected loan was endangered by the high budget deficit, which was nearly twice the ceiling previously set by the IMF. Inflation was expected to increase sharply as the result of an across-the-board 15 percent increase in the price of gasoline and the rates of the state-owned water, telephone, and electric company.

Upon taking office, Calderón warned Costa Ricans that they should prepare for two tough years of austerity measures to solve what he described as "the worst fiscal crisis in the country's history."[2] It was expected that Calderón, despite his populist pretensions, would follow the neoliberal economic policies of the PLN administrations. The appointment of Jorge Guardia, a harsh critic of the PLN's gradualistic approach to structural adjustment, to head the Central Bank indicated that the pace of this conservative economic-adjustment program may pick up during the Calderón administration.

Privatization of the State

The privatization drive underway in Costa Rica entails the transfer of public-sector investment and infrastructure to private corporate investors. It is, however, described by its advocates as the "democratization of property." Since the 1940s the public sector has stood at the center of the country's political and economic development. By the early 1980s one out of every five Costa Ricans in the labor force was working in the public sector.[3] Not only had the public sector vastly expanded since the Calderón Guardia era, so had the cooperative sector which has been amply supported by the government. Cooperatives, most of which are operated like profit-oriented enterprises, accounted for 11 percent of the nation's national income in the mid-1980s.[4]

Public-sector services, while costly, have contributed to the high quality of life in Costa Rica. The state electric company produces most of the nation's electricity from hydropower, and the government-owned telephone company is responsible for a highly automated and efficient system that reaches 80 percent of the population.[5] Government insurance, health care, and social-security services have made Costa Rica one of the healthiest nations in the third world.

But the economic crisis that gripped the nation in 1980 forced a radical cost/benefit reevaluation of many state institutions. Blame for the country's economic difficulties was placed, in large part, on the public sector, which the neoliberal adjusters accused of distorting the economy with its intervention. Privatization has been offered as the solution.

Privatization has appeared in various forms. Its most obvious manifestation has been the opening of the financial sector to private banks. Foreign lending institutions would like to dismantle completely the nationalized banking system, which was set in place in 1949 to guarantee a more even distribution of income and resources. Few in Costa Rica are ready for such a frontal attack on what has been a centerpiece of their society. Nonetheless, the ongoing financial restructuring is steadily eating away at the government banking system and each year placing more funds in the coffers of new private financial institutions.

Selling off state corporations is another facet of privatization. Under a plan financed by AID, the subsidiaries of CODESA, the state development corporation, are being sold to private buyers. Other public-sector institutions have also been threatened with privatization, including the National Production Council (CNP) and the Costa Rican Electricity Institute (ICE).

The third aspect of privatization affects various state service agencies, ranging from road construction and low-income housing departments to the laundry service at state hospitals. Clinics, birth-control services, and agricultural assistance are also being shed by the state and in some cases offered to corporations or cooperatives established by former public-sector employees at government prompting.

Although the privatization process has just begun, the transformation underway is already changing the face and character of Costa Rica. As in austerity programs the world over, it is the poor who are hit hardest by these changes, as the safety net established by the state is surrendered to a private sector more interested in profits than public welfare.

As the process continues, the uneven nature of privatization has become more obvious. Targeted for radical surgery are only those areas of government considered unproductive – meaning that they do not contribute directly to economic growth and the creation of foreign exchange. In contrast, special treatment is accorded that part of the state which (with the blessings and funding of foreign donors) orients services to the private sector, particularly those businesses that produce for export.

An array of government services and financial rewards are directed to new investors, and the government is spending more money on the export-promotion services of CENPRO (Export Promotion Center) and on the creation of export-processing free zones – all the while cutting back the budget of state institutions that benefit the broader Costa Rican society. CEPAS, a social and economic research center in San José, says that privatization "is not simply the dismantling of the state, but the redefinition of its functions."

While strong opposition to privatization emerged among those most directly affected, the government enjoys a surprising degree of public approval for its heralded "democratization of property." Citizens responded positively to claims that privatization of government services will increase efficiency, reduce bureaucratic control, decrease corruption, decentralize power, and even increase democracy. Presented in this way, privatization is understandingly appealing.

Not presented for public discussion and debate, however, are the possible adverse consequences of privatization. Private control is identified with good accounting, efficiency, competitiveness, and lack of corruption. The possibility that newly privatized institutions could be corrupt and inefficient or that their services might be of poor quality or made available only to those who could afford them has not entered into the discussion.

Even critics of privatization acknowledge that at least several state services and institutions, such as CODESA, should be sold. But they also suggest that rather than privatization, what is needed at other public-sector institutions is a thorough housecleaning aimed at making state services more efficient, less costly, and more responsive to public needs.[6] In Costa Rica, privatization must certainly be considered as part of the solution to continuing budget deficits. In the late 1980s, however, privatization came to be regarded not simply as one possible solution but as part of an all-encompassing ideological imperative.

Back to Export Model

Government austerity and privatization are only one side of the restructuring. An equally dramatic revamping of the country's productive sectors is also underway. In accord with the economics of comparative advantage, the IMF, AID, and the World Bank have all insisted that there be an increased effort to promote exports that are competitively priced in the world market. Such items include labor-intensive textiles or electronic goods in the industrial sector and vegetables, flowers, and other nontraditional crops in the agricultural sector. Export fever, which has spread from foreign lending agencies to the government and business elite, was promoted in Costa Rica with the slogan "Exportar es Bueno" (It's Good to Export).

Exports have increased, especially nontraditional ones. But the country still suffers a persistent trade deficit, and the benefits of increased nontraditional exports are counterbalanced by the many economic and social costs associated with the new emphasis on export production. Virtually all nontraditional agroexport production is in the hands of foreign investors, while foreign companies produce all the country's nontraditional industrial exports. This production does mean new sources of foreign exchange, but resulting profits are mostly repatriated. The end products are also heavily dependent on imports that simultaneously deplete foreign-exchange reserves. Growing blemish-free vegetables and flowers in the tropics requires vast amounts of pesticides. Likewise, the income generated by manufactured products must be measured against the cost of the foreign imports needed to assemble these items.

The comparative advantage argument encourages Central American farmers to drop basic-grains production as an unproductive and inefficient venture. But Central American basic grains are to a large extent only uncompetitive when measured against heavily subsidized U.S. grain imports, leaving any country which strictly follows the principles of comparative advantage precariously dependent on continued U.S. grain subsidies and on the whims of U.S. foreign policy.

A further question about any development model defined by comparative advantage concerns the value of the country's labor and resources. To remain competitive, a developing country has to maintain a cheap labor force. But as one Costa Rican critic noted, "If we don't want to live poor, we shouldn't agree to produce cheaply either."

Problems That Will Not Go Away

An infusion of international funds in the early 1980s and a rescheduling of its debt did alleviate Costa Rica's immediate debt crisis. But the problem remains: the country's debt is too high—about $4.2 billion or $1,500 for each Costa Rican—to be repaid. Like other similarly indebted third world countries, Costa Rica has seriously considered declaring a moratorium on debt payments or making payments based on its ability to pay (linking debt payments to export income, for example). Rescheduling of its private debt—about 38 percent of the total—has stalled repeatedly, as creditor banks grow increasingly frustrated by the country's failure to honor its repayment schedules. In the late 1980s, Costa Rica met only 40 percent of its debt servicing commitments to private foreign creditors.

An increasingly attractive option is the sale of its debt at substantially reduced rates to other investors. Taiwan has offered to finance the purchase of two-fifths of the country's foreign debt in exchange for investment and trading privileges. Already, Costa Rica has arranged to have a portion of its debt sold to several international conservation organizations in return for local-currency bonds used to strengthen the country's national park system. These debt-for-nature swaps have erased more than $40 million in external debt. Costa Rica's success in implementing structural adjustment also makes it eligible for the so-called Brady Plan (after U.S. Secretary of State James Brady) of renegotiated debt, under which the IMF and the World Bank would become guarantors of the country's repayment of the reduced debt.

The chief threat to Costa Rica's economic stability and growth is the persistence of the large external debt. Until the debt is dramatically reduced, Costa Rica will be unable to establish a secure foundation for future economic development. Although the debt crisis remains the country's most serious financial problem, it is not the only one. Inflation, large trade imbalances, and the persistent budget deficit also threaten economic stability.

The rising cost of basic goods has severely undermined the enviable standard of living of most Costa Ricans. While structural-adjustment measures have improved trade balances, cut budget deficits, and increased rates of economic growth, living conditions have eroded. As always, structural adjustment affects the poor disproportionately, from reduced corn price subsidies for peasant farmers to higher food costs for low-income urban dwellers. In 1982—during the initial shock of structural adjustments—a crisis developed when the unemployment rate rose to 15 percent. While the number of jobless has declined dramatically, since then inflation, low wages, and reduced government services continue to sound economic alarms for many Costa Ricans.

Some have called the economic turnaround "the miracle of Costa Rica," but other observers are not as impressed. Although an agreement between the CPT (Permanent Worker Council) labor coalition and the PLN government mandated wage raises whenever inflation rises above 7 percent, little has been done by the government to restore workers' income to pre-crisis levels. The minimum wage covers only a third of a family's basic needs, propelling mothers into the labor force and fathers into second jobs. Noting the hardships faced by the working class, the Minister of Economy acknowledged in 1988 that many workers need to spend 100 percent of their wage just to eat. Critics say that if the neoliberal policies persist, Costa Rica will be "Central Americanized" by the end of the century — meaning increased class polarization and conflict.

During the PLN governments the process of structural adjustment in Costa Rica was a gradual one in which the social pact with the poor and working class was not completely forgotten or abandoned. Weighing neoliberal reforms against electoral pressure, the PLN administrations fought off demands from international financial institutions for even harsher austerity measures and a more complete privatization program. In the absence of an alternative plan for economic recovery and progress, it is likely that the neoliberal remedies adopted by the Calderón government will continue to eat away at the benefactor state while trying to increase the rate of economic growth with larger doses of private-sector support — all in the name of economic stability.

Agriculture

Agriculture is the heart and soul of Costa Rica, and its main source of income. About two-thirds of the country's economic activity revolves around agriculture. In the 1980s agriculture underwent an overhaul aimed at making local food production more efficient while increasing agroexports. This "sectoral adjustment," labeled "Changing Agriculture," was imposed by international lending institutions with the consent and approval of the Monge and Arias governments.

The "Changing Agriculture" policy attempted to rectify two weaknesses of Costa Rican agriculture: 1) its overdependence on a few traditional agroexports, namely coffee and bananas, and 2) the perceived inefficiency and backwardness of the local food-producing sector. The government has addressed these concerns from the perspective of free-market and comparative-advantage economics, which is to say that it is promoting agricultural production that is competitive in the international market while reducing its support for nonexport crops.

Encouraged and financed by both the government and international financial institutions, nontraditional agroexport production intensified in the 1980s. Yet virtually all of this new investment is in the hands of individual foreign investors and transnationals. Two transnational corporations—British American Tobacco and Philip Morris—control tobacco production and processing. Del Monte controls most pineapple, mango, papaya, chayote, and lemon exports. Including bananas, Del Monte's agroexports represent 9 percent of the country's total export production. United Brands controls palm oil production and exports, as well as the domestic production of margarine and shortening. Over 80 percent of fern exports, over 50 percent of cut-flower production, and some 40 percent of macadamia nut exports are controlled by foreign investors.

Costa Rica is touted by AID as a success story due to its tripling of nontraditional agroexports in the 1980s. Yet for most Costa Rican farmers, this new emphasis on the production of such nontraditionals as flowers and citrus has represented a challenge to their very existence.

Such issues as commodity prices and quality standards are out of the hands of local producers. Foreign-controlled export houses and traders decide how much and what standard of products to accept, often leaving bewildered farmers stuck with unmarketable produce. Several years ago the World Bank began promoting cocoa production among small farmers, but recently world market prices have nosedived leaving many farmers with large debts and no market for their nontraditional produce.[7] The stress on export crops has also directed credit and technical assistance away from small farmers and to the large commercial-level operations that have easier access to foreign markets.

The result has been turmoil and conflict in rural Costa Rica as basic-grain farmers discover they no longer have access to government credit and price guarantees. Unable to produce profitably under these conditions, these farmers are not planting enough beans, corn, and rice to feed the nation. The resulting food deficits are being met by increased grain imports, some channeled through U.S. food-aid programs. From 1985 to 1988 the production of rice, beans, corn, and sorghum has dropped substantially. Rice production decreased from 244,000 to 157,000 metric tons, beans from 26,600 to 22,800, corn from 126,500 to 97,000, and sorghum from 71,400 to 18,700.[8]

Raising the alarm that the country is losing its food security, farmers have organized to defend their interests and to address the national implications of the "Changing Agriculture" policies. Among their demands are:

* Access to credit for basic-grains production at historically subsidized rates.

* Renewed support for government institutions like the National Production Council (CNP) and the Institute for Agricultural

Development (IDA), which have been hard hit by austerity and privatization measures.

* Price guarantees that permit the profitable production of basic grains.

* Termination of food-aid programs that undermine prices and markets for local farmers.

* More government attention to the technical-assistance needs of grain producers.

* Government commitment to a policy of national food security that relies on local production of staple foods.

The struggle of small basic-grain farmers points to major failings of the country's economic policies, but their protests also highlight the limitations of Costa Rican democracy. Ever since the country began promoting increased agroexport production in the 1950s this sector has been left out of the decision-making process. They have not been the only ones. Agricultural policies have created ever greater numbers of landless peasants, who during the 1980s have become increasingly militant.

The Calderón campaign received strong support among the rural population which had grown frustrated with the agricultural policies of the PLN governments. During the campaign, Calderón appealed to these voters with promises to implement policies to promote self-sufficiency in grains and increase technical assistance and credit for small farmers. His platform for agriculture, if carried out, would satisfy most of the demands of *campesino* organizations that had protested the previous government's policies. Explaining why so many rural voters backed the PUSC campaign, a rural leader in Limón explained, "With Calderón the producers have little to lose and a lot to gain."[9]

As president, Calderón will be faced with the high expectations of the country's small farmers. Even if he wanted to increase government assistance to the agricultural sector, the chronic budget deficit and the restrictions imposed by international financial institutions will make new government funds hard to come by. There is also a question about how sincere his campaign promises really were. Similar promises were made by the Monge and Arias governments while at the same time they proceeded to restructure the agricultural sector along neoliberal lines.

The Rise of Precarismo

"A time bomb is ticking" in rural areas, asserted Rogelio Cedeño of the moderate CCTD labor confederation. "The nation's democratic tradition is in jeopardy because of the government's refusal to heed the call of rural Costa Ricans for the distribution of idle farmland."[10]

The problem of landlessness in rural Costa Rica heated up in the 1960s as the expanding agroexport economy, particularly the beef business, began cornering more of the country's agricultural lands. In an attempt to forestall rural unrest, the government, with the support of AID, created the Lands and Colonization Institute (ITCO), which has since been renamed as the Institute for Agrarian Development (IDA). Rather than pushing through an agrarian-reform program, ITCO concentrated on colonization and titling programs. But the agricultural frontier soon disappeared under the pressure of colonization, and landlessness became endemic in rural Costa Rica.

The response of landless peasants has been *precarismo*, or rural land squatting. It has been estimated that as many as one in six peasant families is part of this squatters movement which targets uncultivated estates.[11] The country's political and economic elite charge that the *precaristas* are "communist inspired" and have overseen harsh repression of the movement.

But the squatting on uncultivated land seems rather to be a type of "spontaneous land reform" rather than a political movement.[12] Given the government's deepening commitment to agribusiness and agroexport production, there is little hope that it will respond to peasant demands for more land with anything more than evictions and repression. In the neoliberal vision, the peasantry represents a backward and inefficient element of the economy that has no place in the modern marketplace and therefore merits no government assistance. At various times, the government has tried to placate the landless with promises for a stepped-up program of land titlization. But far fewer land titles have been awarded than promised, and the budget for the agrarian-transformation institute has been subject to severe cutbacks.

The Dessert Economy: Coffee, Bananas, Sugar

While nontraditionals now account for 30 percent of all agroexports, the main crops are still coffee and bananas. Coffee revenue, which alone accounts for almost 50 percent of the country's agricultural export income, is buffeted by the ups and downs of international prices and quotas. Costa Rica, however, is favored because of its high-quality coffee and ideal growing conditions. Two government institutes regulate the coffee industry: ICAFE controls coffee exports and allocates quotas among coffee mills, while the Ministry of Economy sets domestic prices and minimum wages for coffee pickers. Like their counterparts throughout the third world, Costa Rican coffee producers are worried that the 1989 demise of the quota system of the International Coffee Organization will mean lower prices and no guaranteed market. They point to the problems faced by cocoa growers who also operate without the guarantees of international quotas and have recently been hit hard by falling prices and international surpluses.[13]

In the 1980s foreign investors began to exert more control over the coffee sector. Liberalized laws allowed foreign traders to finance local exporters and processors, facilitating the purchase of shares in domestic exporting companies and coffee mills. Foreign companies which gained influence during the 1980s include Volkart, Jacobs, Lonrays, and Ruthfos. Together with local investors, Volkart opened the country's most modern coffee mill, Beneficio 2000, in late 1988.

Banana production occupies second place among agroexport crops. Foreign companies, led by RJ Reynolds (Del Monte/BANDECO) and Castle & Cooke (Standard Fruit/Dole), dominate the industry. Local growers account for about one-third of production, but foreign companies control the packaging and export stages. In 1984 United Brands withdrew from its banana plantations on the Pacific coast, leaving most banana production along the Atlantic coast. In 1988 BANCOL, a Colombian multinational, bought about 3,000 acres for banana production. Bananas from Costa Rica are shipped mostly to the United States (57 percent), West Germany (28 percent), and Italy (12 percent).

The sugar industry has regained its vigor with the rise in international prices and an increase in U.S. sugar quotas. Virtually all sugar exports go to the United States, and Costa Rica has also begun to export sugar-based ethanol to the United States.

However, shrinking markets in the United States combined with rising production costs have precipitated a severe slump in the beef industry, which emerged about 1970 to meet rising U.S. demand for cheap, lean beef. In response, reproductive herds have been reduced, resulting domestically in higher prices and decreased consumption. While local beef consumption is declining, broiler production and chicken consumption have boomed. "Chickenburgers," from poultry fed on imported yellow corn, are sold at the many fastfood outlets in San José.

The forestry industry is facing a crisis that is in many ways self-induced. Ironically, while the Costa Rican government has been forward-looking in its creation of national parks, it has exercised few controls over deforestation. Despite new government regulations, the high deforestation rate continues. An incentive system does encourage private landowners to reforest, but the system encourages the planting of fast-growing trees rather than the precious hardwoods that are disappearing. As a result, the country may experience a shortage of wood for domestic use by the mid-1990s.

Industry and Finance

Costa Rica's industrial sector developed in the 1960s largely as a result of the Central America Common Market, which gave manufacturers a larger market for their goods. The country has two general categories of industrial investment: one which produces mostly for the local or regional market and another which simply uses Costa Rica as an export platform for textile and electronic goods produced with cheap, unorganized labor.

The first category has benefited from what are known as import-substitution tariff protections that afford it a sheltered market to produce and market its products. This industrial sector is now resisting structural-adjustment measures that threaten the protected status of import-substitution industry. It calls for a slower pace of adjustment and for low-interest, government-guaranteed loans to help make local industry more competitive regionally and internationally. The second category also benefits from government incentive and tax-exemption provisions designed to attract foreign companies to the country.

The fastest-growing manufacturing industries are food-processing, beverage, and tobacco companies which are largely controlled by U.S. transnational corporations. Companies that depend on a high degree of imports have been adversely affected by devaluation and other restructuring measures that erode the protections under which companies catering to the internal market have thrived. Increased prices for imported petrochemicals have also resulted in a slowdown in the domestic production of chemical products, including fertilizers and insecticides.

The government reports over 700 foreign firms doing business in Costa Rica. These range from companies manufacturing fishing lures to those assembling lingerie and costume jewelry under drawback incentive provisions. Some one hundred companies operate under the drawback provisions of the U.S. 807 temporary admission program that permits companies to import assembled goods (like jeans and other clothing whose pieces are sewn together by foreign labor) duty-free into the United States. About 30 companies are located in the country's five Free Zones, where they benefit from having their workforce trained at the government's expense, either on or off the site. The textile industry has boomed in recent years. Between 1986 and 1988 the textile industry increased its number of workers from 14,000 to 35,000.[14]

Under the provisions of the Caribbean Basin Initiative and new government measures to attract foreign investors, there has been a small boom in foreign manufacturing investment in Costa Rica. Virtually all of this industrial production is of the export-processing variety, meaning that there are few local inputs aside from labor and that the assembled goods are destined for foreign markets. In this investment climate, Costa Rica has become a world center for brassiere manufacturing, with companies like Maidenform and Lovable managing the international assembly and marketing arrangements. About one-fifth of the new ventures in the manufacturing sector are from the Far East, mostly Taiwan.[15]

Tourism is the country's third major source of foreign exchange, after agriculture and industry. After a drop dating from 1979, the country is again filling up with tourists, and there is new foreign interest in tourism investment. This new mini-boom is attributed to the international attention given to Costa Rica as a result of Arias' Nobel Peace Prize and to recent favorable international publicity about the country's national park system.

Privatization of the Finance Industry

The dust still has not settled after the government — under pressure from AID, the IMF, and the World Bank — opened the door to private banking. As predicted by some, a number of private banks opened shop only to bilk depositors of their savings certificates and then collapse. As a result of all the interest in private banking by foreign donors, these banks are swimming in credit they cannot get rid of. There are four government banks and about 20 private ones. The state banks retain a monopoly on checking and savings accounts although private banks can now accept time deposits. Like banking, the insurance industry was also nationalized long ago, and all insurance is issued by INS, the state's insurance company.

Chapter 4

Society and Environment

Popular Organizing

Costa Rica does not have the tradition of popular organizing seen elsewhere in Latin America. The government's attention to the basic needs of poor and working people has in many ways obviated the need for the kind of community organizing that occurs in countries where there is little government concern for the broad social welfare. Popular organizing in other Central American countries was sparked, to a large degree, by progressive Catholic clergy, who recognized that traditional charity solutions fell far short of addressing the structural problems facing poor communities. In Costa Rica, the church hierarchy has isolated itself from the progressive trends within the Latin American church and has vigorously discouraged social activism on the part of its clergy.

Church organizations like Catholic Action, which in other countries organized cooperatives and sponsored popular-education programs, remained paternalistic charitable institutions in Costa Rica. To a certain degree, the government's involvement in the popular sector has been an attempt to undermine popular organizations established by the Popular Vanguard Party (PVP) in the 1930s. Rural organizations and associations promoted by the government were, at least in part, a response to the PVP's history of its associations of banana workers and its attempt to form Peasant Leagues, and the government's establishment of community-development associations was an attempt to undermine the communist-sponsored Progressive Community Directorates.

Beyond simply providing social services, the government, and to a lesser degree the Catholic church, has created institutions that channel and control community organizing. In the cooperative sector, the government maintains influence over cooperative organizing through two autonomous institutions: the Cooperative Bank and INFOCOOP (Institute for Cooperative Promotion). Cooperatives began developing in

Costa Rica in the 1950s and expanded greatly in the 1970s. Many in government have seen cooperatives as an appropriate vehicle for broad-based community development, but government-sponsored cooperatives often function as instruments to undermine pre-existing popular organizations.

There are three basic kinds of cooperatives: consumer, productive, and credit. Most cooperatives are more like capitalist businesses than true cooperatives where work and profits are shared. Government austerity measures have hit the cooperative sector hard, forcing many into bankruptcy as government subsidies are cut back. Particularly hurt by reduced government support are those rural cooperatives that produce basic grains while those producing for the export market or marketing such luxury items as cheese have been less hard hit.

Community groups are integrated into a network controlled by a state institution called DINADECO (National Directorate of Community Development), which channels government resources and training to local groups known as Community Development Associations. Increasingly, however, more and more community groups are demanding genuine decision-making power and independence within this government-financed structure.

In the early 1980s there was a surge of popular organizing as a result of the economic crisis. Groups marched through San José demanding that utility rates not be raised, social services not be cut, and for more low-income housing to be built. These protests forced politicians to recognize that if structural-adjustment measures were pushed forward too fast the government would be facing widespread social unrest. The PLN successfully pacified organized popular opposition by promising to contain food costs, increase housing construction, and lower proposed rate increases. During the Monge administration, the most vocal protests concerned the need for low-income housing.

Accordingly, the Arias government which followed focused its efforts in this area in order to demonstrate the state's continued attention to the needs of the poor. In the process, one of the most vocal popular organizations, COPAN, was incorporated into the government's housing bureaucracy, losing its independent voice and militancy — having made a deal with the government to direct no land occupations in return for a minor role in the administration of low-income housing. While the Arias government did demonstrate more concern for low-income housing, cutbacks in other areas of government assistance, to which there had been less popular reaction, were not restored. Imitating these methods, President Calderón and the PUSC political party also adopted a popular tone in the 1989-1990 electoral campaign, promising an expanded housing program, the creation of a national family institute, and the provision of subsidies for the poor.

Another response to the popular movement by the Arias government was an initiative to promote the creation of a National Confederation of Community Development Associations. Some community leaders opposed the idea of a national confederation out of their concern that it would become another instrument used by the state to control the popular movement. Such a confederation would likely also face widespread disinterest among members of community-development programs.[1]

The debilitated state of the union movement has prevented it from playing a leading role in sparking popular opposition to the neoliberal onslaught. Only the *campesino* associations have mounted any serious response to the government's new economic policies. It was in the agricultural sector where the consequences of restructuring became quickly apparent. As a result of the new economic thinking, the country began to experience food deficits, and peasant producers were squeezed out of the farming business by pricing and credit policies. At the same time, policies promoting agroexport production had the effect of driving small producers off the land, creating a large and increasingly militant sector of landless *campesinos*.

At the head of the agricultural sector's popular movement in the late 1980s was the National Agricultural Union (UNSA), a coalition of some two-dozen associations of basic-grain farmers, both large and small. In September 1986 and again in 1987, farmers took their protest to San José. The march in 1986 was met with severe repression not often seen in the streets of the capital city but increasingly common in rural areas. In 1987 the protesting *campesinos* organized a hunger strike. They presented the government not only with their complaints but also with a proposal for an alternative policy that requested balanced agricultural development which assists the process of crop diversification while guaranteeing national food security. In 1988 UNSA member organizations blocked several major highways and occupied government buildings to demonstrate the seriousness of their demands. The coalition gradually dissipated, however, as large producers made their own arrangements with the government.

In the three years that this dynamic rural movement was developing, the farmer associations proved adept not only at bringing medium-size and some large farmers into the coalition but also at attracting some of the more conservative and government-linked associations of small farmers. This unity, while an indisputable strength, has been difficult to maintain and fortify due to the government's strategy of negotiating with farmer groups sector by sector. The government has also tried to isolate the most militant farmer associations, notably UPAGRA (Union of Small Farmers of the Atlantic), by accusing them of being Marxist-organized and -financed organizations with military capabilities.[2]

While the primary focus of the peasant movement has been government structural-adjustment policies that emphasize nontraditional exports, a growing factor in rural Costa Rica is the movement of landless peasants demanding land. In their takeovers of uncultivated private land and challenges to the government's Institute for Agrarian Development (IDA), landless *campesino* families have been met with escalating repression, both from private and official security forces.

The economic situation for Costa Rica's lower classes exacerbated during the 1980s, but this economic trauma did not necessarily broaden and strengthen the country's popular movement. This was due in part to the ability of the government to at least partially alleviate the concerns of the most vocal sectors. Another factor debilitating the popular sectors is the political sectarianism that divides community organizations, especially during election years. The lack of a strong tradition of community organizing, especially in urban areas, and a low degree of popular political education also explain the weak state of the popular movement.

The *campesino* movement has been the most militant and unified sector of the popular movement since 1986. Its militancy and increased radicalization reflect the government's lack of serious attention to its demands. As the movement has developed, its demands have broadened to include more than just specific sectoral concerns. The entire neoliberal trajectory has come under *campesino* criticism. The movement's ability to catalyze widespread opposition to these policies is limited, however, by its own tenuous unity and the deep divisions in style and perspective that separate urban and rural Costa Ricans.

Reflecting on the state of popular organizing, political analyst Manuel Rojas Bolaños observed, "The popular movement does not appear willing to endure more restrictions [austerity measures and budget cuts], but since they lack an appropriate alternative, they move like blind worms, which upon running into tiny obstacles remove some of them while others force them to redefine their route, without ever knowing where they are going."[3]

Labor and Unions

The state of union organizing highlights yet another of the apparent contradictions in Costa Rican society. Although workers are not subject to the kind of repression seen in other parts of Central America, the union movement is weak and in decline.

Historically, unions linked to the Communist Party have been the strongest and have paved the way for the entire movement. Despite close links with the church, government, and foreign donors like the American Institute for Free Labor Development (AIFLD), the social-democratic elements of the union movement have remained weak with a strong base only in the public sector. Internal divisions, the inability to formulate a common political/economic vision, and the rise of the *solidarismo* movement presented major obstacles to the debilitated Costa Rican labor movement of the 1980s. In Costa Rica, workers are generally better paid than their counterparts elsewhere in the region, but wages are still one-fourth to one-third the U.S. average.

The labor movement can be traced to the last century when workers formed mutual-aid societies and the government began regulating workers and professionals. In the 1890s the Catholic church took an interest in labor organizing as a way to form a popular base for the Catholic Union Party. Later the church supported labor unions mainly as an antidote to the mounting strength of communist labor unions. The country's first strikes and open labor conflict involved Chinese and Italian workers contracted in the 1880s to build the country's railroads.

It was not until 1913, with the formation of the General Confederation of Workers (CGT), that the country gained its first bona fide labor organization. The Communist Party, formed in 1931, pushed labor organizing to new levels of militancy and success, beginning with the 1934 strike that brought United Fruit to a standstill. The communist-backed Costa Rican Workers Confederation (CTCR) grew steadily, giving the party major influence in national politics. Pressure from the leftist unions resulted, for example, in the institution during the 1940s of the country's Labor Code, including protective guarantees and a system of bonuses and severance pay.

Since the mid-1940s two interrelated forces — social-democratic tendencies associated with the AFL-CIO and Social Christian elements associated with the Catholic church — have struggled to undermine the influence of the Communist Party among the nation's working class. The church, for example, organized the Rerum Novarum Costa Rican Workers Confederation (CCTRN) in 1945 to withdraw worker support from the leftist-backed CTCR. The international department of the AFL-CIO, in close cooperation with the CIA and U.S. State Department, soon established links with the anticommunist CCTRN. Then, after the victory of social democrat José Figueres in 1948, the CTCR was dismantled and the Communist Party outlawed. At the same time, Figueres and the new government promoted the CCTRN (later reorganized as the CCTD). An international network comprising the AFL-CIO-associated Inter-american Regional Organization of Workers (ORIT) and the AID-financed AIFLD also threw its considerable support behind the CCTD.

Leftist unions were not permitted to operate again until 1953, at which time the Costa Rican General Workers Confederation (CGTC) was established. Once more, it was the unions associated with the reconstituted Popular Vanguard Party (PVP) that began to dominate the field of trade-union and peasant organizing as the CCTRN gradually crumbled. The Catholic church lost interest in the formation of Christian unions after the death in 1952 of Archbishop Sanabria. For its part, the PLN, while favoring the CCTRN and later the CCTD, did little to promote trade unionism.

Benefiting from the conciliatory policies of the reformist state and by national economic growth, the union movement grew steadily in the 1960s and 1970s. The strengthening of the organized labor was impressive, rising from just 2.6 percent of the workforce in 1963 to 15.7 percent two decades later. Those advances were largely lost in the 1980s, with only 10 to 15 percent of the labor force currently belonging to unions. The strength of the labor movement, even at its height, was undermined by its concentration in the public sector and virtual absence in private industry. By the late 1980s only 6 percent of the private-sector workforce was organized. Costa Rican unions were strong only in the large public sector, where half of government employees are union members. Another sign of the weakness of Costa Rica unionism is its lack of strike activity. In 1987, for example, there were only five official strikes, just one of which involved the private sector.

The labor movement is characterized by the proliferation of small unions and the lack of labor unity. The country has over 350 unions and seven union confederations. These confederations represent less than three-quarters of union members since 27 percent belong to independent unions.[4] Among the strongest independent unions are the National Teachers Association (ANDE), the country's most powerful labor organization with some 26,000 members. In 1987 ANDE joined with two smaller teachers' unions to form the Inter-Magisterial Council. The Public Sector Workers Union (ANEP), with some 10,000 members, is another major independent confederation and has ties with the communist unions. The country's labor confederations and their affiliations are as follows:

The **Permanent Worker Council (CPT)**, formed in 1986 and comprising the six largest union centrals, is the latest and most successful attempt at labor unity. CPT's members include: Costa Rican Confederation of Democratic Workers (CCTD), Confederation of Costa Rican Workers (CTC), Authentic Central of Democratic Workers (CATD), United Workers Central (CUT), National Confederation of Workers (CNT), and Costa Rican Workers Central (CTCR).

The **National Confederation of Public Sector Professionals (CONPROSEP)** is a confederation that represents public-sector unions.

The **Costa Rican Confederation of Costa Rican Workers (CCTD)**, with a membership of some 16,000, is an affiliate of the International Confederation of Free Trade Unions (ICFTU) and politically close to the PLN. In the mid-1960s CCTD shed its ties to the Christian labor movement in favor of its association with the ICFTU and AIFLD.

The **Authentic Central of Democratic Workers (CATD)** formed in 1971 in a split with CCTD over alleged interference by ORIT/AIFLD advisers. CATD renounces external ties, is based in San José, and includes several public-sector unions.

The **Unitary Confederation of Workers (CUT)** was established in 1980 as a confederation of all unions and smaller confederations. Its domination by the Popular Vanguard Party (PVP) and the General Confederation of Costa Rican Workers (CGTC) resulted in the social-democratic unions leaving the coalition. As a result CUT soon became little more than a new name for the CGTC. Associated with the Communist Party and the World Federation of Trade Unions (WFTU), CGTC emerged in the 1950s from the remnants of the CTCR and the CGT. The confederation won legal recognition in 1953 and draws its strength primarily from railroad, port, and banana workers. Its power was substantially eroded by the failure of long strikes against Del Monte and United Fruit in the early 1980s. In 1984 CUT was further weakened by a split in the Communist Party, which resulted in the formation of a rejuvenated version of the old CTCR.

Formed in 1983 by AIFLD organizers wary of the increasing independence of CCTD, the **National Confederation of Workers (CNT)** is seeking ICFTU affiliation. Justifying its horse swap, AIFLD charged that CCTD had entered into "opportunistic alliances of convenience with the Communists" and was following a policy of "short-sighted hostility" to the Monge administration. Through its Campesino Strengthening Project, AIFLD works with CNT to support a peasant organization called

FEDETAICO, which promotes nontraditional agroexport production by conservative *campesino* groups.

The **Confederation of Costa Rican Workers (CTCR)**, once revived by CUT, later estranged itself from its erstwhile cohort through a formal break in 1984, the result of a split in the PVP. The new CTCR allied itself with the PVP split-off called the Costa Rican People's Party (PPC).

The **Costa Rican Workers Central (CTC)** was formed in 1972 as an evolution of Social Christian unionism, which formally took hold in 1964 at the initiative of the Latin American Confederation of Workers (CLAT), an international affiliate of the World Confederation of Labor (WCL). With about 8,000 mainly rural members, CTC has allied with CCTD to mount an "anticommunist offensive" against the Labor Unity Committee (CUT).

Obstacles Facing Labor Unions

As the labor movement enters the 1990s it faces an array of obstacles, including the following:

* Effective loss of worker rights to collective bargaining.

* Restrictive government policies.

* Constraints imposed by the country's Labor Code, whose benefits are applicable only to those labor conflicts judged legal by the Supreme Court.

* Rise of the *solidarismo* movement.

* Lack of effective labor movement unity.

* Continued ability of government to coopt sectors of the labor movement.

Collective bargaining is waning as a method for resolving labor conflicts. The most severe blow to collective-bargaining rights came in 1979 when the government passed the Public Administration Law which restricts the right of public employees to negotiate contracts. While the government has respected unions that predated the 1979 law, it has steadfastly refused to recognize the rights of new public-employee unions to negotiate contracts. Direct agreements between workers and companies in lieu of collective-bargaining arrangements are common in the private sector. The government has further restricted the strategy options of public-sector unions with the 1984 Financial Stability Law which additionally narrows the few instances when government institutions can negotiate directly with their employees.

Another threat to public-sector employees comes from the privatization of the government institutions for which they work. This issue is pressing since some 30 percent of the country's labor force and 65 percent of organized labor falls within the public sector.[5] Leading the opposition to privatization are workers of the Costa Rican Electricity Institute (ICE).

The founding of CPT in 1986, coalescing all the labor confederations, represented labor's strongest commitment yet to unity and common defense. But the Arias government proved adept in negotiating separate agreements with the public-sector associates of CPT. Although the agreements guaranteed certain protections against further wage deterioration, they offered no hope for the recuperation of real wages lost since the beginning of the economic crisis. Critics faulted CPT for its failure to lead the fight against the neoliberal restructuring that undermined hard-won social reforms.

Heartened by the populist tone of the Calderón campaign, the labor movement was hoping for a cooperative relationship with the new government. Promises made by the candidate Calderón to revise the Labor Code, encourage the participation of workers in the profit-sharing schemes, and to adjust wages according to inflation won him the support of many workers. According to Gilbert Brown, CNT's secretary general, Calderón entered office with a great commitment to the popular sectors.[6]

The first pronouncements of the new labor minister signaled a labor policy more conservative than the PUSC's platform. Rather than reforming the Labor Code to strengthen the right to organize unions and bargain collectively, the labor ministry announced its intentions to revise the code to facilitate the growth of the *solidarista* movement. Deepening austerity measures, massive layoffs of public-sector workers, and the failure of negotiated wage increases to match inflation rates set labor at loggerheads with the new government.

The economic and labor policies of the Calderón government has spurred protests from organized labor. But the debilitated labor movement has little mobilizing power. What gains it made during the Arias administration came mainly from pacts arranged with the government rather than through protests and strikes. With the PUSC having no organic links with the labor sector, negotiating with the Calderón government has proved less fruitful.

Solidarismo Takes Off

Solidarismo is a philosophy of worker-owner cooperation formulated by Alberto Marten in Costa Rica in 1947. It is designed as an alternative to class confrontation, unionism, and collective bargaining. In practice, *solidarismo* takes the form of financial associations in which businesses and workers alike contribute to the formation of credit cooperatives and investment projects. The funds come from worker savings and investment by the company owner of the employee's future severance pay.

As a result of rapid growth in the 1980s, the *solidarismo* movement now includes more than 1,100 associations with over 140,000 members and accumulated capital of over $30 million. The base of the movement has been the manufacturing sector in the San José metropolitan area, but since 1985 *solidarismo* has also made impressive inroads in the agricultural sector, especially the banana industry. The movement is also surging in the commercial sector, and lately has even established associations in the public sector. Over 90 percent of the country's U.S.-based transnationals, including Firestone, McDonald's, Coca-Cola, RJ Reynolds, IBM, and Standard Brands, sponsor *solidarista* associations.[7]

During the 1980s the number of *solidarista* affiliates doubled, while the union movement stagnated. By the end of the decade, *solidarismo*, which included 16 percent of the workforce, could rightly boast that its members outnumbered the rival union movement.

Solidarismo comprises two tendencies. One emanates from the John XXIII Social School directed by Father Claudio Solano, a conservative Catholic priest. This faction of *solidarismo* likens the movement to the social philosophy of the Catholic church and has focused on the manufacturing and banana transnationals in Costa Rica. It sees *solidarismo* as a "holy crusade" against communist-inspired unionism and class struggle. With a staff of over four-dozen organizers, the school not only helps organize new associations but also is a center for training for the entire movement.

One reason *solidarismo* is growing so fast is the foreign financial support it is now receiving. It not only receives supports from transnational corporations but also from such sources as the U.S. embassy, the Konrad Adenauer Foundation, and the U.S. Agency for International Development (AID). In 1985 the school received an AID grant of 1.8 million *colones* which was channeled through ACORDE/CINDE (See Nongovernmental Organizations) to sponsor 74 courses to train over 1,800 Costa Rican workers in the principles of *solidarismo*.[8] In addition, representatives of FINANSOL, a *solidarista* finance company, said in 1989 that FINANSOL had been promised AID credits. Additionally, the John XXIII School has received regular donations from the U.S. banana companies. The Catholic church's support of the John XXIII School indicates the degree to which the church has retreated from its earlier strong support for the principles of unionism.

The other *solidarista* current, founded in 1980 and backed by Costa Rican entrepreneurs, is known as the Costa Rican Solidarista Union (SURSUM). Unlike the John XXIII School, SURSUM does not promote the purported religious foundations and objectives of *solidarismo*. SURSUM's position is that unions advocate class struggle while solidarity associations promote "not a class struggle but a solidarity among men."

In 1988 strong opposition to *solidarismo* arose from the World Congress of International Confederation of Free Union Organizations (ICFTU), a conservative, social-democratic confederation with which the AFL-CIO is associated. The ICFTU charged that *solidarismo*, as practiced in Costa Rica, violated the standards set by the International Labor Organization (ILO), especially in regard to workers' rights to union membership and collective bargaining. While the U.S. government has favorably regarded and even financially supported *solidarismo*, it has also traditionally supported the operations of ICFTU, causing a mild dilemma for foreign policy makers.

The Costa Rican labor confederations joined together in 1987 to create the National Union Commission on Solidarismo (COSNAS). Unions have also done extensive research and analysis of their adversary through the Service Commission for Labor Growth (ASEPROLA), labor's main source of information about *solidarismo*. Opposition to *solidarismo* has grown not only in response to *solidarismo*'s own growth but also in reaction to the movement's increasingly aggressive attempts to undermine unions by collaborating with unionized companies and by functioning as unions themselves in arranging direct wage agreements with employers. Unions complain that companies fire unionized workers, for example, to make way for *solidarista* associations.

Solidarismo also faces internal opposition as members of *solidarista* associations complain that the associations are undemocratic and lack adequate financial controls by worker representatives. Some observers predict increasing radicalization among the associations as companies fail to live up to promises to protect worker interests and as workers fall further and further behind in wage levels and in the quality of working conditions. There is also concern building among the *solidarista* associations that some companies may never be able to give retiring workers their severance pay due to poor investments and bankruptcies. One critic quipped, "*Solidarismo* is like Alka-Seltzer. Once the initial fizz is gone, the workers will be left with an empty glass and a flat taste in their mouths."[9]

Yet the benefits of *solidarismo* have not been all illusory. Aside from the reluctance to involve themselves in labor-management strife, workers often choose and stay with *solidarista* associations for some tangible rewards. They point to the cheap loans, savings plans, social events, and development programs offered by the associations.

From its base in Costa Rica, *solidarismo* is spreading north to Guatemala, Honduras, and El Salvador. In 1985 the Supreme Solidarista Council of the Americas, based in Guatemala, was founded to promote *solidarismo* throughout the region. Organizers from the John XXIII Social School have traveled throughout the region as part of organizing campaigns sponsored by area business owners. The regionalization of *solidarismo* has received essential backing from such rightwing political leaders as William Middendorf (director of the Middendorf Commission for Peace and Economic Justice in Central America and a member of the Committee of Santa Fe, a conservative U.S. policy institute) and Curtin Winsor, Jr. (ambassador to Costa Rica, 1983-1985).

Winsor, dubbed the "ambassador of *solidarismo*," heralded the movement as "perhaps the most original and significant ideological Latin American contribution to the West."[10] Both Winsor and Middendorf have been at the forefront of a drive to promote *solidarismo* as both an economic and ideological paradigm for Central America, and for such other geopolitical hot spots as the Philippines and South Africa. In particular, they encourage the integration of stock-ownership and profit-sharing plans into the *solidarismo* movement to hasten its trajectory.

The union movement slowed down in the 1980s while experiencing several major setbacks, notably the switch of many banana workers to the *solidarismo* movement. Unionists looking for hopeful signs can find them in the achievement of a certain degree of unity through the CPT and the success of some unions in winning limited demands. As a whole, though, the union movement is characterized by a lack of both militancy and of a strong political analysis of the national crisis.

Schools and Students

Costa Ricans enjoy the best public education system in Central America. Government expenditures on education as a percentage of national income are 1 percent higher than the 4 percent standard recommended by UNESCO. As one result of this commitment to education, 93 percent of Costa Ricans are literate.

A qualitatively superior system of higher education also distinguishes Costa Rica. For the last few decades, there have been two university systems: University of Costa Rica (UCR) and National University (UNA) as well as the state-financed Technological Institute of Costa Rica (ITCR). Costa Ricans also have easy access to the State University at a Distance (UNED), a state extension/correspondence university established especially for students living in rural areas. Like many other Latin American nations, university-level institutions enjoy legal autonomy. This autonomy, which ensures freedom of expression and political activism, has been carefully observed, in contrast to other countries of the region.[11]

On the whole, post-secondary education in Costa Rica is of a higher quality than primary and secondary education, where learning is by rote. A recent study, for example, found that 80 percent of students in sixth, ninth, and eleventh grades did not receive minimum passing marks on Spanish-language examinations. Although literacy is widespread, the average citizen has only an eighth-grade reading level.[12]

Recently, however, private institutions of higher learning have mushroomed. Most are very expensive, concentrate on business and the sciences, and are run like corporations. The Autonomous University of Central America (UACA), founded in 1975, is the leading private university. Actually, it is a collection of different departments (law, medicine, etc.) which function as separate profit-making enterprises. Founded by former UCR professor Guillermo Malavassi, UACA was hailed as a pro-capitalist institution in contrast to the left-leaning sentiments that characterized the national centers of higher learning during the mid-1970s. Today, UACA continues to be a center for neoliberal thought, joined by an array of other private colleges, most of which also foster conservative views about education, politics, and economics. These include National University (based in San Diego), Interamerican University of Puerto Rico (based in Puerto Rico), Higher School of Business Administration (ESAN), Higher Institute of Business Administration (ISAE), Technical Institute of Business Administration (ITAN), and numerous others.

The student movement in Costa Rica began to take hold in the mid-1960s and reached a high point of social activism in 1969-1970 when university students mobilized to oppose a government mining contract with the aluminum mining company ALCOA. This successful struggle against environmental destruction and economic exploitation was the most dramatic example of a new student and faculty activism that lasted into the late 1970s. Demands of student organizations targeted the national budget for education but also included such social issues as higher salaries for university workers, banana-union strikes, and *campesino* struggles. By the turn of the decade, student activism had begun to wane, and the control of the universities by leftist students and professors was dealt a final blow by the mounting internecine conflicts within the Popular Vanguard Party (PVP), which had gained influence within the FEUCR student organization.

In the 1980s the student movement was largely quiescent and dominated by conservative elements. Concerns about entertainment predominated discussions within student organizations, while concerns about regional problems were dismissed as "leftist" issues. Whereas leftist students in the 1970s were very critical about the activities of moderate Christian groups on campus, the university campuses of the 1980s were eager hosts to numerous rightwing U.S.-based evangelical organizations, including Campus Crusade for Christ (Alfa y Omega).

Government austerity measures have, however, sparked some student unrest. Budget cuts forced UCR to lay off more than 400 employees and raise tuition, which led to a student march in October 1987 to demand a budget increase for higher education. The rector of the university criticized the government for allowing higher education to pass into private hands, a trend, he warned, which may make a university education a privilege enjoyed only by the elite.

Viewing the proliferation of private universities as a threat to continued public funding for the state system of higher education, students and professors at UNA, UCR, and ITCR have voiced strong opposition to plans by AID and the Kellogg Foundation to create a new, private agricultural school in the country. The planned Agricultural School for the Humid Tropics School (EARTH) is unnecessary and unwarranted, assert opponents of this project, as it will duplicate facilities that already exist within the country and because it falls outside the state system.

Media

Costa Rica enjoys a free press, but it is dominated by the ideological right. While there is no censorship or suppression of the press in the country, it is difficult to find news that is not filtered through the stridently rightwing convictions of the owners of the major media.[13] The nation's largest daily newspaper, *La Nación*, sets the tone and direction of most news coverage in Costa Rica with its circulation of 75,000 every morning.

La Nación is more than a newspaper. It is a media complex. It publishes a half-dozen magazines, including the prominent *Perfil* and *Rumbo*, and is linked to the cable station Cablecolor. Stockholders of *La*

Nación also hold interests in the daily newspaper *La República*, Radio Monumental, and Radio Mil.

The directors and staff of *La Nación* have been directly tied to the extremist Free Costa Rica Movement (MCRL), a rightwing civic group with a paramilitary wing.[14] News of the MCRL appears frequently in the paper. *La Nación* was also close to the Nicaraguan contras and served as a voice for their cause throughout Latin America. It distributed a weekly supplement called *Nicaragua Hoy*, directed from Miami by Pedro Joaquín Chamorro (son of the former editor of *La Prensa* who was assassinated for his anti-Somoza views and of Violeta Chamorro, the new U.S.-backed president of Nicaragua). Pedro Chamorro refused to disclose the funding sources for *Nicaragua Hoy*, but Edgar Chamorro, a former contra leader and the editor's distant cousin, charged that the supplement was CIA-financed.

La Nación is the country's preeminent source of news and opinion. The other media, especially the radio and television news, follow the lead of *La Nación* in reactions to news events and public policies. This is a phenomenon that close observers call the "news of consensus" in Costa Rica.

Sharing this conservative consensus are the two other dailies, *La Prensa Libre* and *La República*. Both newspapers emerged as alternatives to *La Nación*, but have moved to the right since their founding and now share its uncompromising conservatism. The morning paper *La República*, for example, was founded in the 1950s to provide an alternative to the anti-Figueres focus of *La Nación*, and now has a circulation of 55,000 and is slightly less conservative than *La Nación*. *La Prensa Libre*, an afternoon paper with a circulation of 45,000, appeared in the 1960s as an second alternative. The ideological cohesion of the press represents the degree to which the most reactionary elements of the capitalist class have come to dominate the country's information business. An example of the extent to which the media goes to undermine the credibility of those who differ with its worldview was the repeated publication by *La Prensa Libre* in 1988 of reports claiming that the country's *campesino* organizations were really "paramilitary, subversive" organizations.

Three smaller papers—*Semanario Universidad*, *Esta Semana*, and *The Tico Times*—offer a more liberal view, but their influence is limited by their relatively small circulation. *Semanario Universidad*, the official paper of the University of Costa Rica, has gained an international reputation for its coverage of politics and the arts. It is characterized by its anti-imperialist and distinctly leftist editorial stance. *The Tico Times*, owned and edited by Richard and Dery Dyer, was established as an English-language weekly to serve the *pensionado* and tourist communities. In recent years, the paper has distinguished itself by its investigative reporting in such areas as women's issues, pesticide use, the role of AID, and the contra presence in Costa Rica. A *Tico Times* reporter, Linda Frazier, was killed in the bombing of contra leader Edén Pastora's press conference in May 1984. In late 1988 the newsweekly *Esta Semana* appeared on the stands, and was welcomed by many Costa Ricans tired of the sharply skewed reporting and analysis of the three dailies. There are two communist weeklies, *Libertad* and *Adelante*.

Radio stations abound, yet offer little diversity, relying on regurgitated news from the three dailies. Radio Reloj boasts the most listeners, and it bolsters the conservative consensus sweeping Costa Rica with its daily news programs and its influential noon editorial called *La Opinión*. The news station Radio Monumental is at least as conservative, and faithfully reflects the rightist opinions of its owners. An exception to the conformity of the radio news is the Sunday morning program *La Patada* on Radio Sonora, which offers criticism in a humorous vein and a wide array of viewpoints. Many radio stations carry Voice of America (VOA) and other U.S. Information Service (USIS) programs in Costa Rica, including Radio Costa Rica which devotes about half its broadcast time to VOA programming. VOA's *Buenos Días, América*, is fed to 28 radio stations in Costa Rica, while some 17 stations broadcast other VOA package programs.

Radio Costa Rica was established in 1984 as a VOA transmitter station in Costa Rica with U.S. Information Agency (USIA) funds. It was operated by the Costa Rican Association for Information and Culture, a conservative group of investors convened by the U.S. embassy. A principal figure behind Radio Costa Rica is Rodrigo Fournier, the director of Channel 2 television. The establishment of this VOA transmitter in northern Costa Rica at Quesada for the first time allowed the VOA to offer AM broadcast band service to any part of Central America. The broadcasting from Quesada covered northern Costa Rica and portions of Nicaragua, including Managua. In late 1989 VOA announced it would no longer be broadcasting through Radio Costa Rica, but that VOA programs would continue to be broadcasted to Costa Ricans on another frequency.

Another strong voice for the contras was Radio Impacto which, according to Edgar Chamorro, was bought by a contra support group in Venezuela. Like Radio Costa Rica, the CIA-backed Radio Impacto broadcast deep into Nicaragua and in 1989 also devoted considerable attention to Panama.

Ideological variety in the world of radio was severely undermined by the 1980 bombing of a new radio station that provided listeners with international news from a leftist perspective. The most liberal station currently broadcasting is Radio América Latina, which has proved responsive to the concerns of the popular movement.

Over 90 percent of Costa Rican households have one or more television sets, on which they can receive a half-dozen local stations and foreign cable programming. Cablecolor, the local cable service, broadcasts the U.S. government's daily *Amet* program as well as CNN's 24-hour news service. Channel 7 leads the others in terms of viewers, and is trying to assert full control of the medium through the professionalization of its *Telenoticias* news program. Channel 7, formerly owned by ABC, is of the same ideological stripe as the major print media, as is its major competitor Channel 6 which is known for its rightwing prattle. Channel 13, a station founded by the then-ruling PLN, also provides a more liberal interpretation of the news as well as offering an array of cultural programming. According to USIA, most audiovisual material offered to Costa Rican TV stations is readily placed.

A restrictive press licensing law in Costa Rica has been denounced by the Inter-American Press Association (IAPA) and condemned as a human rights violation by the Inter-American Court on Human Rights. Under the controversial law, press licenses are issued only to graduates of the University of Costa Rica's school of journalism and certain approved foreign universities. The law is strongly backed by the Costa Rican Journalists Association, which issues the licenses. Locally, the press licensing law is opposed by *La Nación* and other media, including *The Tico Times*.

Carlos Morales, a professor at the school of journalism and the editor of *Semanario Universidad*, defends the measure as a way to ensure professionalism, minimize cultural imperialism, protect the rights of journalists, and empower the journalists association. President Arias also strongly endorsed the compulsory licensing of journalists in what was seen by some political commentators as an effort to strike a blow at *La Nación*, a long-time opponent of Arias' PLN party. "How much better society feels," explained Arias, "if it knows that he who boasts a degree in journalism is a university professional." However, the salutary effect of press licensing, which has been on the books since 1969, is open to debate, given the poor quality of Costa Rican journalism.

The penetration in the 1980s of the media by the CIA and USIA raised concerns among many Costa Ricans. In an affidavit submitted to the World Court, former contra leader Edgar Chamorro testified that he had personally paid Central American journalists with CIA funds and was told by the CIA that the agency was bribing Costa Rican journalists to disseminate U.S.-produced information about Nicaragua and the contras. Carlos Morales charged that at least eight journalists, including three top editors, received monthly CIA payments.[15]

A continuing source of tension within Costa Rica is the investigation by U.S. journalists Martha Honey and Tony Avirgan into the 1984 bombing in the Nicaraguan border village of La Penca. Avirgan and Honey contend the CIA planned the bombing attempt on the life of Edén Pastora with the involvement of hardline contra supporters in Costa Rica. In mid-1987 the Costa Rican Democratic Association, an ultra-right group, brought suit against the two foreign journalists, accusing them of being spies. About the same time, Avirgan and Honey were also arrested for receiving a package of cocaine, supposedly sent by Nicaragua's Minister of Interior Tomás Borge. According to the journalists, the CIA has assisted the Costa Rican Democratic Association and that the cocaine was sent by people working for the CIA.[16] In addition, they also claim that the CIA carried out the 1984 bombing. Both cases against the journalists were dismissed. For years, Honey and Avirgan came under fire from the conservative press. Recently, however, the papers have published several editorials saying that evidence indicates that the CIA was indeed involved in the La Penca bombing which killed three journalists and injured a dozen more, including Avirgan.

The progressive community in Costa Rica commonly refers to what they see as the ideological domination and control of the country by the rightwing media. "In Costa Rica, we don't have repression with bullets, we have control by the news," observed *Semanario Universidad*'s Carlos Morales.

To a large extent, journalism in Costa Rica bears the stamp of the USA. The country mission of USIS, with an annual budget of $3.5 million (excluding the VOA budget) is the largest in Central America. USIS distributes a wide variety of video programs and biweekly *Telecommunications Update* to the local channels in addition to transmitting programs such as the *State Department News Media Briefing* through the USIS' WorldNet satellite delivery system. The 17 USIS staffers in Costa Rica also work closely with the local print media, distributing a regular packet of news articles to editors. Journalists in Costa Rica are being brought to the United States as part of a $12 million educational program for Central American reporters.

Health

The good health of Costa Ricans — superior to that of many communities of the United States — is a product of a state-sponsored infrastructure of health services matched in Latin America only by Cuba. When compared with most other Central American countries, the advances in health made by Costa Rica are truly impressive. One indicator of the country's commitment to citizen health is its social security system, which covers three of every four Costa Ricans — easily the highest rate in the region. Latest statistics show infant deaths to be fewer than 18 per thousand compared with 79 per thousand in Guatemala. Life expectancy is high (74 years for males and 76 for females), a rate matched in Central America only by Panama.[17]

In the 1970s rapid progress was made in national health. Early in the decade, the government promised to modernize the health system so that low-cost health care would be available to all Costa Ricans. Acting on this resolve, the nation's hospitals were nationalized and health care personnel integrated into a national medical system that reached out for the first time to rural areas. The government also greatly extended social-security health coverage to most citizens, regardless of income or occupation.

By the end of the decade, the health and welfare of Costa Ricans had improved markedly, far outstripping all its northern neighbors. Four of five Costa Ricans were covered by social security-sponsored health care, communicable diseases were eradicated, infant mortality had dropped by 69 percent, and deaths from infectious and parasitic diseases fell by 98 percent between 1970 and 1980. So successful was the health care campaign in the 1970s that AID took Costa Rica off its eligibility list for health care assistance because the country had become too healthy.[18]

While the 1970s were an era of progress, the 1980s were a period of cutbacks and regression. During the 1970s the expenses of the Social Security System (CCSS) had risen by almost 700 percent — a big reason why the government was experiencing chronic budget deficits.[19]

The country's public health care system came under not only economic pressure but also ideological attack in the 1980s. Businesses, who were obligated to pay a higher percentage of their payroll into the CCSS, began to call for the reprivatization of health care. In this call for privatization, they received the support of foreign agencies like AID. In 1982 AID's *Health Sector Policy Paper* lambasted the government for its subsidized health services while advocating private-sector medical care and fee-for-service medicine.[20]

Structural adjustment and austerity measures during the 1980s took a serious toll on health service. The Family Assistance Agency, a welfare and community development organization, was hard hit, suffering a budget reduction of one-third. The lack of funds reverberated throughout the health system, affecting disease-prevention programs, child centers, feeding programs, and the installation of sanitary systems.

The statistics are not yet in for the 1980s, but health professionals predict a sharp decline in the nation's health status. Signs of this deterioration include a rise in contagious diseases such as measles and meningitis, an increase in cases of hepatitis and diarrhea, and outbreaks of malaria and sexually transmitted diseases.

Hospital directors and Social Security and Family Assistance officials state that the quality and availability of health services have substantially deteriorated over the last ten years. Medicines and hospital beds are in short supply; medical care, when available, has become routine and dehumanized. At least 10 percent of hospital patients acquire new diseases during their hospital care due to budget cuts in hospital sanitary services.

The shrinking welfare budget has also meant less government money for potable water systems, sewage treatment, and public health programs. As a result of the fewer wells and community water facilities being installed, the percentage of Costa Ricans with potable water and sanitary facilities inside their homes is declining for the first time. The lack of public funds for trash collection and sewage treatment has translated into increased water contamination. This has meant a general decline in public health and a rise in preventable diseases. By 1985 the government itself acknowledged that increases in gastrointestinal diseases, alcoholism, and drug dependency were directly attributable to the economic crisis and deteriorating social conditions.

While water and sanitary systems in Costa Rica still compare favorably with other Central American countries, there are wide gaps in service. Some 50 percent of the homes in San José are not connected to sewage lines, and only 30 percent of the sewage/trash collected in the country is treated chemically. Outside the San José metropolis, the state of public health and sanitary services is considerably worse. Mortality rates, for example, are 50 percent higher in rural areas, indicating the limits of the country's welfare state.[21]

The privatization of the health-care system advocated by the business elite, and to a lesser degree by AID, has been only partially implemented. Those with the ability to pay have found private health-care service. For the poor, however, the decrease in government health services simply mean no access to health care. The government—pressured by unions, leftist political parties, and the PLN's social-democratic wing—has tried to minimize budget cutting in health care. But as medical anthropologist Lynn Morgan observed: "The Costa Rican government's challenge will be to perform a political high-wire act: maintaining state control over the health system developed during the 1970s while not exceeding the austerity budget of the 1980s, yet without reducing services at a time when people need them the most."[22]

Religion

Roman Catholicism is the dominant religion in Costa Rica. The Catholic church is also the society's most powerful institution after the government itself. While its base has been seriously undermined in the last 20 years by the evangelical movement, Catholicism still functions as the *de facto* state religion. The Catholic church played a central role in shaping the social-democratic ideology in Costa Rica. It has been instrumental in legitimizing the social-welfare state, maintaining a lid on popular organizing, and propagating an ideology of anticommunism.

The development of the modern church can be traced back to 1940 when Monsignor Sanabria became Archbishop of San José and brought with him a new vision of the church's role in society. Under Sanabria's reign, the church promoted several charitable and activist lay organizations including Catholic Action, Young Catholic Workers (JOC), and the Confederation of Costa Rican Workers Rerum Novarum. This new social activism of the church coincided with the Social Christian reforms promoted by the Calderón government in the 1940s, and the archbishop was drawn into an unlikely alliance with the government and the communist Popular Vanguard Party in backing these social reforms.[23]

With the ascent of the PLN in the 1950s, the Catholic church once again withdrew from the political arena, while still supporting the Figueres government. This new political conservatism and the country's isolation from progressive trends within the Latin American church became evident in 1968, when the Archbishop of San José abstained from signing the Medellín document, which affirmed "the option for the poor." The social concern and intellectual vigor of the Sanabria tenor were lost to history. Instead, anticommunism became the prevailing theme of church homilies—despite the lack of a real threat within the country. The hierarchy, as part of this hardened anticommunism and suspicion of social activism, discouraged and at times denounced those members of the clergy who associated with the popular movement. At the end of the 1970s

the conservatism of the Costa Rican church stood in marked contrast to
the revitalization of the church in many other parts of Central America.
According to Andrés Opazo Bernales, the author of *Costa Rica: La Iglesia
Católica y el Orden Social*, the following tendencies distinguished the
church at the turn of the decade:

* Lack of attention to social problems (for example: unemployment
  and high cost of living) generated by modern capitalist development.

* Close cooperation with the state in social work, characterized by the
  church's paternalistic nature.

* Support of a spiritualist approach to religious belief, in contrast to
  the more socially rooted theology promoted by the Medellín
  Conference.

* Suppression of dissidents within the church.[24]

The advent of domestic economic crisis and political upheaval in the
region pushed the Catholic church in Costa Rica out of its lethargy into
assuming a more active social and political role. With the appointment of
Monsignor Román Arrieta as archbishop, the church once again became
an active ally of the PLN-controlled government under Monge and Arias.
The church recognized that social problems had to be addressed if society
was to remain stable, yet it chose to address the deepening economic crisis
with charity rather than suggesting structural changes. As Opazo Bernales observed, Arrieta, a long-time PLN activist, talked more about social problems but always within the context of the PLN and the reformist
government. In Costa Rica, the "option for the poor" mandate was translated into increased charity and government reforms.

Harmony between rich and poor and between church and state has
been the ideology promoted by the church hierarchy. Its endorsement of
the *solidarismo* movement, its promotion of such welfare organizations
as CARITAS, and the integration of Catholic clergy into government institutions like INFOCOOP (the government's cooperative institute) exemplified this cautious theology. Arrieta entwined the church in the
national politic, appearing routinely alongside of the president and placing the power and credibility of the church behind the government. It also
provided strong backing for the government's and the media's condem-
nation of the Sandinistas.

While the church's ties with government strengthened in the 1980s, its
hold on Costa Rican society has waned. As elsewhere in Central America,
Catholics in Costa Rica are eclectic believers, whose most fervent expres-
sions of faith are evoked during Holy Week and at the baptism, marriage,
or death of family members. Over 80 percent of Costa Rican Catholics

do not attend mass regularly.[25] Cultural Catholicism has not been able to resist the rise of the evangelical movement, spearheaded by pentecostals. To some degree, however, the incursion of evangelical churches into traditional Catholic territory has spawned a charismatic movement that incorporates the emotionalism and personal renewal aspects of pentecostal faith into Catholicism. Within the Catholic church, there do exist communities and clergy that espouse a theology of liberation, but the institutional church isolates and represses this tendency while promoting a more spiritualistic religion.

Rise of Evangelical Movement

Evangelical churches,[*] which accounted for 1 percent of Costa Ricans in 1949, made rapid advances since 1965 to encompass about 16 percent of the population by the mid-1980s.[26] These churches spread throughout Costa Rica from their 19th century base among the West Indian population of the Atlantic coast.[27] Today, the predominant evangelical churches are the Assemblies of God, Seventh-Day Adventists, Pentecostal Holiness church, Church of the Nazarene, Association of Bible Churches of Costa Rica, Association of Christian Churches, and the Fundamentalist Baptists. There are over 115 different evangelical organizations in the country, most of which have experienced significant growth in the 1980s. In San José, the number of evangelical congregants doubled between 1983 and 1986.[28]

Three mainline Protestant denominations — Methodists, Baptists, and Anglicans — have the longest history in Costa Rica (dating from the mid-1880s) but currently comprise only a small group of followers. Beginning in the 1890s, U.S. missionary Bible societies began setting up missions among the Spanish-speaking society. In addition to the Central American Mission and the Latin American Mission, the Seventh-Day Adventists also established missions at this time, and are today one of the largest evangelical churches in the country.

The Latin American Mission, which entered the country in 1921, was the driving force in exposing Costa Rica to the evangelical movement. Its sponsorship of Billy Graham's Caribbean Crusade in 1958 and the Evangelism-in-Depth campaign in 1961 had the effect of establishing evangelical faith as a credible alternative to Catholicism. Latin American Mission also contributed substantially to the creation of an evangelical infrastruc-

---

[*] In keeping with its usage in Central America, the term "evangelical" is used here to refer to all non-Catholic Christians, including pentecostals, fundamentalists, and mainline Protestants.

ture in Costa Rica, having founded numerous institutions including the Latin American Biblical Seminary, the national evangelical radio station TIFC ("Lighthouse of the Caribbean"), and the Bible Clinic, as well as the Association of Bible Churches.

The recent boom in evangelicalism in Costa Rica, however, is the direct result of advances by pentecostal churches, mainly Assemblies of God, Church of God, and the Pentecostal Holiness church, which have been setting up churches since the early 1950s. Besides altering the theological mix in the country, pentecostal growth also has resulted in rival Catholic and more traditional evangelical churches adopting many of the tactics and emotional nature of the pentecostals.

In the 1980s the evangelical movement penetrated the wealthier sectors of Costa Rican society through para-ecclesial organizations. These include Full Gospel Businessmen's Fellowship, Women's Aglow Fellowship, and Ministry to the Student World (MINAMUNDO). Such rightwing U.S.-based evangelical organizations as Campus Crusade for Christ (Alfa y Omega), Globe Missionary Evangelism, Trans World Missions, Maranatha (New Jerusalem Christian Association), Christian Growth Ministries (publishers of *New Wine Magazine*), Navigators, and CBN's 700 Club have also recently begun operating in the country, particularly among the middle and upper classes.

Yet with all the evangelical sects to be found in Costa Rica, the country has not been subjected to the massive evangelization campaign by pentecostals and fundamentalists experienced by countries like Guatemala and Honduras. One explanation is that Costa Rica has not suffered the same kind of natural catastrophes and political crises that tend to attract such groups.

Costa Rica has been adopted as a regional center for many evangelical institutions including Latin American Mission, the evangelical education organization Alfalit, Difusiones Interamericanas (which provides broadcasting services), and the Latin American Evangelical Center for Pastoral Studies (CELEP).

Generally, evangelical churches exert a conservative, pro-U.S. influence in Costa Rican society. In the late 1960s and early 1970s a politically and theologically progressive faction of evangelicals did emerge, forming a base within the Biblical Seminary. But this new dynamism of ecumenism and religious social activism was eventually marginalized by most U.S. missionary societies, and has been largely unsuccessful in gaining a strong following among the evangelical community. A spokesperson for the ecumenical CELEP blames the conservative tenor of Costa Rican evangelicalism on the United States. "Costa Rica is the ideological front for the United States in Central America," she complained, "Fifteen years ago, there used to be an ecumenical movement here, but it was destroyed."

Outside this evangelical movement are numerous other religious groups, most of which have their origin in the United States. These include the Mormons, Jehovah Witnesses, Theosophical Society, Baha'i, Hari Krishna, and Unification church.

Nongovernmental Organizations

Nongovernmental organizations (NGOs) involved in development, business, and charitable activities proliferated in Costa Rica in the 1980s. Three main factors explain this rapid increase in nonprofit humanitarian and developmental activities: 1) a response to the government's failure to address deteriorating social and economic conditions, 2) the new attention to the NGO sector by AID and other foreign funding agencies, and 3) a tendency to locate regional NGO headquarters in Costa Rica due to its relatively stable and pleasant setting.

NGOs, both local and international, began emerging in the 1960s. The most prominent local NGO established during the 1960s was the locally based Private Voluntary Federation (FOV), which provides coordination and support for mainly women's charitable organizations. Throughout its history, FOV has received important financial and technical assistance from AID and the U.S.-based Overseas Education Fund (OEF). The widespread availability of government social services and the country's international status as an advanced developing country meant, however, that the NGO sector was quite small before the 1980s.

In the 1970s and early 1980s AID channeled some of its development aid to the government's own community development organization called DINADECO. (See Popular Organizations) But later involvement emphasized the privatization of all development assistance. Beginning in 1985 AID began to increase its financial support of and direct involvement in the NGO sector. Through CINDE, a business NGO created and funded by AID, the agency began to channel funds to a growing number of NGOs. In 1987 CINDE/AID officially established ACORDE as a funding and coordinating organization for NGOs. The AID Mission selected the members of ACORDE's board of directors. All are members of the country's business and professional elite with no previous NGO experience.

ACORDE operates on an annual budget of $3.8 million, all of which came from AID. The bulk of ACORDE's budget is still underwritten by AID local currency funds, with another large portion (about $1.2 million) from an AID grant to a U.S. NGO called Private Agencies Collaborating Together (PACT), which is virtually fully funded by AID. In 1989 ACORDE also began receiving grants from groups in West Germany (Hanns-Seidel Foundation and Agricultural Action), from the U.S.-based Resource Foundation, and from the Inter-American Development Bank (IDB). It is actively seeking additional European and Canadian funding.

The formation of ACORDE parallels similar efforts by AID in other Central American countries to fund and coordinate NGO operations. The PACT representative in Costa Rica confided that AID created ACORDE as a "funding window" for NGOs and that it is now "the only show in town when it comes to getting big bucks for NGO work." According to the PACT representative, "The AID director, Dan Chaij, strongly supported ACORDE because he thought that the AID economic-stabilization program for Costa Rica was certain to impoverish some people and that ACORDE could help reduce the social impact of AID policies." ACORDE was created as a "shock absorber."[29]

ACORDE's funding priorities mirror AID's own priorities. The emphasis is on profitable productive projects, not social assistance. One approach of ACORDE-sponsored projects is co-financing operations with private companies. Coca-Cola, for example, will co-sponsor an ACORDE project and be able to stamp its name on the development project. Besides providing funding and technical assistance to NGOs, ACORDE also aspires to a more influential role within the NGO community itself: promoting itself as an NGO clearinghouse, playing a leading role in forming a regional NGO umbrella group, and sponsoring training events for NGOs.

AID's money goes to the more conservative NGOs in Costa Rica. Excluded from the AID-triggered NGO boom is a network of highly effective and innovative Costa Rica NGOs which sponsor popular education, community development, and research projects. These organizations (such as CENAP, CEDECO, and ALFORJA) rely mainly on European funding. ACORDE has not been bashful about expressing its political objectives. As a former ACORDE director observed, "We don't want to have happen in Costa Rica what happened in Nicaragua." The expansion of ACORDE has created resentment among a number of Costa Rican NGOs, notably FOV, which feel that ACORDE with its conservative, business focus has undermined independent NGO organizing.

In addition to its work with ACORDE, AID also funds numerous U.S. NGOs in Costa Rica, including: Action International (AITEC), Agricultural Cooperative Development International (ACDI), American Institute for Free Labor Development (AIFLD), CARE, Catholic Relief Services (CRS), Heifer Project International, International Executive Service Corps (IESC), OEF, Pan American Development Foundation (PADF), Partners of the Americas, Planned Parenthood, Salvation Army, Technoserve, and World Wildlife Fund.

In addition to those NGOs funded by AID, there are numerous local NGOs that count on funding from a variety of Canadian and European donors as well as a few that receive private U.S. support. Many of these groups are involved in popular education programs and are members of Council of Promotional and Popular Education Centers. The Center for Development Training (CECADE) offers valuable technical services to NGOs sponsoring popular education activities.

Unlike other Central American countries, where social conditions are more serious, the NGO sector in Costa Rica does not serve, along with the churches, as society's safety net. The social infrastructure set in place by NGOs and churches elsewhere in the region is the public sector domain here. As these government-sponsored welfare services are cut back, though, churches and NGOs are gradually moving into this type of social-assistance activity. Nevertheless, most NGOs continue to focus on specific objectives, such as family planning, business development, and technical assistance.

Women and Feminism

In its class character and articulated gender focus, the women's movement in Costa Rica resembles feminism in developed countries. Issues such as sexual preference, battering, job discrimination, and sexual harassment are publicly debated in Costa Rica. Employment of women in government has been quite impressive. Women have occupied many cabinet-level and even vice-presidential posts in sharp contrast to most of Costa Rica's Latin neighbors. Even though some were believed to be lesbians, they were not only tolerated but respected for the quality of their work. There are numerous feminist organizations, such as Centro Pro-Mujer and CEFEMINA (Center of Feminist Action and Information), which maintain a gender focus in their education and organizing. There are, however, few links between the women's movement and social-justice issues and struggles in Costa Rica.

As early as 1984 the country had a shelter for battered women, in contrast to the other Central American countries, none of which have established one. Another indication of the degree to which women's rights is a concern in Costa Rica is the ongoing effort to pass an Equal Rights Law. The country already has a highly advanced Family Code which stipulates that a husband and wife have equal rights and equal duties. The code also provides equal recourse to divorce for men and women, and allows divorce by mutual consent, thereby avoiding emotionally wrenching court cases.

Although women's rights are increasingly becoming part of social consciousness in the country, the overall situation of women has not greatly improved. The continuing economic crisis has apparently resulted in an increase in cases of woman battering, up over 200 percent since 1983. Child abuse rates are also rising. While men are guilty of most child sexual abuse, mothers are largely responsible for other physical abuse. Social worker Ana Virginia Quesada explained, "Women are the main perpetrators of physical abuse, possibly as a power assertion on the lines of 'the boss kicks you, you kick the dog'."[30]

Rape has also increased, but convictions have remained few, in part due to a Costa Rican law which requires proof that a rape victim physically resisted her attacker. "In Costa Rica we live with the myth that this is a peaceful society," observed Sara Sharratt, a professor of women's studies at the National University. "We are so busy thinking about no army that we ignore the fact that there is widespread, institutionalized violence against women in this 'peaceful' society."[31]

Higher prices and lower wages in recent years have also resulted in an increase in the percent of women in the registered labor force (currently about 28 percent). Women generally receive lower wages than men, and the rate of women working for less than minimum wage is 3 times the male rate.[32] The film documentary *Dos Veces Mujer* (Two Times a Woman), produced by a female Costa Rican director, powerfully portrayed the problems faced by women breadwinners. In urban areas, the average income for working women is about half that of men. Numerous projects exist to provide productive employment for women living in poor urban areas. Most of these projects, however, are cottage industries in which women sew clothing for substandard wages. One such project sews the clothing used to dress up Barbie dolls for export to the United States.

The Costa Rican government has a history of financing and otherwise encouraging women's organizations. It has supported the FOV, a women's social-service organization, and in 1975 legislated against the sexist use of women's bodies in commercial advertising. Although male officials have often proved initially responsive to women's demands, there has been little real commitment to guarantee women's rights. The measure against sexist advertising, for example, has not been enforced, and the government's Institute for Agricultural Development (IDA) has only rarely given land titles to women, despite their central role (often as single parents) in many *campesino* families.

For the last two decades, sterilization has been the second most common form of birth control for women. According to the Ministry of Health, 25 percent of Costa Rican women are sterile. Yet sterilization is illegal; and its legalization as a woman's choice has been strongly opposed by the Catholic church, which says that legalized sterilization would be the first step toward legalized abortion.

Birth control in Costa Rica is a nationalistic and feminist issue, as well as a religious one. Many critics say that foreign agencies like AID and Planned Parenthood are undermining the sovereignty and dignity of Costa Ricans with their birth control campaigns. They point out that many Costa Rican women were sterilized without their consent in the 1950s. Many Costa Rican feminists, however, assert that sterilization, like other forms of birth control, is their right. As a Costa Rican feminist publication stated: "Women don't choose sterilization just because they are ignorant or are forced without consent. Social problems such as lack of employment, education, decent housing, medical services, and safe, secure contraception are decisive factors."[33]

The decrease in social services and the worsening economic conditions for the poor may account for the alarming incidence of adolescent mothers in recent years. Public health officials estimate that every 52 seconds a teenaged girl gives birth. One-fourth of all Costa Rican women have their first child between 15 and 18 years of age, and 40 percent of the female adolescent population is not in school. One-fifth of these teenagers now work as maids. These statistics indicate that previous advances in education and equal opportunity won by Costa Rican women may now be reversed by the new economic and political climate.[34]

Native People

Costa Rica is a largely *mestizo* society but with lighter skin tones than those of other Central American countries — a trait explained by the historic absence of a widespread native population. Today, there are fewer than 25,000 Indians in the country, most of whom live within the 22 Indian reserves established by the government. The majority of Costa Rican Indians occupy isolated stretches of jungle near the Panamanian border, although other reserves are found further north along the Pacific coast. As in other parts of tropical America, the surviving Indian population of Costa Rica has evolved from a tribal to a peasant society.[35]

Not only are these Costa Rican natives isolated from the dominant society, they are isolated from each other, both by their geographical seclusion and by their own cultural differences. A dozen ethnic groupings exist within the small Indian population, although only six native languages have survived the last five hundred years of colonization. As isolated as most Costa Rican Indians may be, they have been reached by the dominant culture of the country. While they may live without electricity and running water, Costa Rican Indians do live in a culture of soft drinks and junk food, and battery-powered TVs are commonly found on the reserves.

Costa Rica boasts a progressive policy regarding its native peoples. In 1977 the government passed the Indigenous Bill establishing the right of Indians to land reserves and authorizing measures to preserve native culture and language. Not simply paperwork, the bill has resulted in government programs to promote Indian culture and to introduce bilingual education for Indian students. But numerous Indian community leaders complain that the government has not adequately protected Indian land rights and treats the Indian people solely as a tourist attraction. As Baldomero Torres, a member of the Cabagra community, commented, "We don't want to be treated as animals in a zoo, but we do need help to improve our poor living conditions."

While the government is given much credit for promotion of Indian culture, it gets few good marks when it comes to preserving Indian land rights. On many reserves, the majority of land has fallen into the hands of "white" Costa Ricans. Non-Indian cattle ranchers and farmers have seized and fenced Indian land with impunity. Indians living in the extensive Talamanca Reserve, which straddles the border with Panama, are also threatened by increasing land speculation, mining, and petroleum exploration. The Cabécar and Bribri Indians, the largest ethnic groups in the country who make their homes in the Talamanca mountains, are widely scattered in migratory family units and have not formed the kind of political and social organizations that could better protect their lands and their culture against encroaching outside interests.[36]

Economic development is an issue that now confronts the Indian communities of Costa Rica. At a time when many are taking steps to preserve their culture from further deterioration, they are also being faced with decisions about how to best promote their economic interests. A case in point is a controversy that has surfaced in Talamanca. Opposition has arisen there to the development projects of the AID-financed New Alchemists Association (ANAI), whose objective is to transform the agricultural practices of peasant farmers, chiefly by introducing the production of nontraditional crops. One Indian group called the Cultural Committee charged that ANAI representatives are foreigners who "come to teach us how to use medicinal plants which they cannot have known before they arrived here." The committee also noted, "We have thousands of years of experience of living based on agriculture, and we know much better which are appropriate soils to plant in, as well as the moon cycles to coordinate the planting." But other Indians in Talamanca and other communities stress economic development over cultural traditions.[37]

Black Costa Ricans form the major non-indigenous minority group in the country. Concentrated on the Atlantic Coast around Puerto Limón, they are the descendents of slaves brought from the West Indies in the late 1800s to help build the railroad through the highlands and later to work on the banana plantations. Their lifestyle is very similar to that of the British West Indies, and they speak a Creole English and are commonly members of the Anglican church. Victims of racial discrimination, the Costa Rican blacks have been isolated from the country's political and economic life. Increasingly, however, the country's black community is gradually assuming the Spanish language and culture as its own.

Refugees

Over the last couple decades, Costa Rica has served as a haven for Latin American political exiles. But it was not until the late 1970s, when thousands of Nicaraguans crossed the border to escape the widening repression unleashed by Somoza, that Costa Rica gained its present status as host to large concentrations of Central American refugees. Most of these Nicaraguans returned to Nicaragua after the Sandinistas' victory over Somoza in 1979, but their numbers were soon replaced by Salvadorans fleeing the escalating violence in that country. With the heating up of the contra war and later as economic conditions worsened in Nicaragua, tens of thousands of Nicaraguans once again sought refuge in Costa Rica.

As of early 1989 there were 43,000 documented refugees in Costa Rica, although only some 7,000 were living in the country's half-dozen refugee camps sponsored by the United Nations High Commission on Refugees (UNHCR). Included in this official refugee population are some 6,200 Salvadorans, 2,500 Cubans, 200 Guatemalans, 75

Panamanians, and 25 Hondurans. Over 33,000 Nicaraguans have refugee status in Costa Rica. In addition, 150,000 to 200,000 undocumented refugees – most of them Nicaraguans – have found a temporary home in Costa Rica.[38] The Salvadorans who sought refuge in Costa Rica entered the country in the early 1980s. Most were women and children, and had personally experienced the terror of military counterinsurgency campaigns. The Salvadoran community in Costa Rica, which has been treated with both suspicion and caution by the government, has been prohibited from most forms of political activism and protest.

Immediately following the electoral defeat of the Sandinistas in February 1990, pressure began building in Costa Rica to close the refugee camps and deport those Nicaraguans illegally living in the country. By mid-1991 the United Nations had closed its refugee camps and 2,500 Nicaraguans still legally in Costa Rica were in the process of being repatriated. Reflecting its almost exclusive concern with Nicaragua, the Costa Rican government observed in April 1991 that there was no longer a need for refugee services since "armed conflicts have practically disappeared from the region."

Environment

Costa Rica has the reputation in Central America for having taken the boldest steps to protect its environment. In many respects, this reputation is well deserved. The government is committed to protecting nearly a quarter of its national land area in national reserves and has recently instituted a logging moratorium. A series of environmental laws have been instituted to protect the country's extraordinary genetic diversity, which includes some 850 bird species and 1200 types of orchids. The Costa Rican citizenry certainly lead the region in terms of environmental consciousness. Alexander Bonilla, one of the country's most outspoken environmentalists, has even been trying to form a Costa Rican Ecology Party.

Focus on Costa Rica by such international environmental organizations as the World Wildlife Fund and Nature Conservancy have also contributed to the country's reputation for environmental concern, as well as the presence in Costa Rica of an influential community of foreign-born environmentalists, notably the Quakers and their sponsorship of the Monteverde reserve. Credit for the nation's national park program must also go to Olof Wessberg and Karen Morgensen, who from their home in the remote Nicoya Peninsula began pushing for a national park system in the 1960s.[39]

Though the environmental movement achieved significant gains in the last 15 years, laws and good intentions have fallen short of effective protection and improvement. While legally established wildlands occupy some 25 percent of the country's land base (11 percent in national parks and 14 percent in protective status), less than one-half of this area is adequately protected. As a consequence, the reserves are eroding at the edges of the national parks. The desire to clear land for farming and cattle-grazing spurred until recently one of the world's highest rates of deforestation. The country has been losing about 106,000 hectares of forest each year — a rate which means Costa Rica would have no wildlands outside its national parks by the year 2000. The government's Ministry of Mines and Energy has warned that Costa Rica may be importing wood within a decade if the deforestation rate continues.

More than 25 percent of the watershed of the Pacific coast region has been seriously eroded due to deforestation. It has been estimated that Costa Rica loses about 680 million tons of soil to erosion each year. As a result, some areas even suffer incipient desertification. Watershed deterioration as a direct result of deforestation presents an additional threat to the country's hydroelectric system, which produces most of the country's electric power. Reservoirs are silting up at a rapid rate due to soil erosion, costing the system hundreds of millions of dollars in lost revenues.

The government itself has contributed to extensive deforestation by encouraging frontier colonization by landless peasants, many of whom had been pushed off their land by the expansion of sugar and cattle industries. About three-fourths of the land acquired by the government's Institute for Agrarian Development (IDA) between 1961 and 1985 was forested.[40]

Despite legislation, the destruction caused by reckless economic development has continued apace. In 1987 the government did temporarily prohibit new logging, but it is widely acknowledged that logging continues despite the ban. In addition to the timber industry, agriculture and ranching have posed the primary threats to the country's remaining forests. In the past 35 years, pasture land has doubled in Costa Rica, now covering some 40 percent of the national territory.

Pesticide abuse was previously concentrated in the traditional agroexport crops like bananas and sugar. Yet with a new focus on nontraditional exports, the major threat lies in uncontrolled pesticide use by producers of vegetables and flowers. Agricultural chemicals have all but exterminated armadillos, fish, and crocodiles along the Tempisque River. Humans also fall victim to pesticides. One study found that between 1978 and 1983 the number of farm workers poisoned by pesticides increased steadily, up to almost 800 cases a year. Since the country has no government agency — though one has been proposed — that monitors food products for harmful chemicals, consumers are not currently protected from pesticide contamination.

For the last quarter-century, urban sprawl across the Central Valley has been spreading concrete over the country's most fertile region — an agricultural heartland distinguished by rich volcanic soil and low-relief terrain. The San José metropolis now covers about 3 percent of the national territory and holds about 50 percent of the population. Spreading out from San José, uncontrolled urban growth is consuming vegetable and dairy farms. If growth rates continue, this area could house up to 1.8 million people by the year 2000, and in the process destroy some of the richest coffee-producing land in the world. Streams that intersect this exploding metropolis are already clogged with trash and wastes.

Uncontrolled dumping on an industrial level is also a major environmental hazard. Contamination of Pacific coast waters near Puntarenas by government fertilizer plant (FERTICA) effluents is one example of the lack of sewage and dumping regulation. Along the same coast around Quepos and Golfito, the banana companies have made a habit of dumping their toxic waste into the ocean.[41]

The government's efforts to create a large national park system stand at the center of the country's commitment to environmental protection. International conservation organizations have joined this effort through what has been called the Debt-for-Nature Swap program. These organizations (including the Nature Conservancy, World Wildlife Fund, and the World Fund for Flora and Fauna) purchase some of the nation's external debt from foreign banks, usually at less than 20 percent of face value. The government's Central Bank then buys this debt with short-term government bonds, with the stipulation that the funds be used for conservation. More than $40 million has been invested in this innovative manner of debt settlement.

Some critics charge that the Debt-for-Nature Swap fuels inflationary tendencies while reducing pressure for debt restructuring. National sovereignty is also at stake in a program that allows international organizations to make resource-planning decisions rightfully made by governments themselves. For the most part, though, the debt swaps have been widely applauded as a way to stop the continued destruction of the environment, although the small scale of the financial agreements do not make them a real alternative to serious debt restructuring.

A major trend in protecting ecosystems is the plan to consolidate about two-dozen protected areas into seven "megaparks" over the next five years. The unofficial prototype for this plan is the Guanacaste National Park, the creation of which is largely due to the efforts of U.S. ecologist Daniel Janzen. Janzen's ambitious campaign to establish the Guanacaste park has made him a very high-profile individual both within Costa Rica and international environmental circles. His power in shaping government conservation policy has created deep resentment among the staff of the national park system.

The integration of peasants and communities living within or on the borders of national parks into park planning and development has been another trend that distinguishes environmental protection in Costa Rica. The Minister of Natural Resources called this concept "mixed management," which he said means "managing buffer zones as integral to the protected area, teaching rural people agroforestry, and training them as tourist guides."

One forest preserve that has experienced serious environmental damage is the Osa National Park, which has been invaded by gold miners. Despite a governmental plan to buy out the fortune seekers, the problem persists, resulting in silted waterways and mercury contamination. Another threat to the environment in the Osa Peninsula is the increased access to the isolated region as a result of a road- and bridge-building effort in the region sponsored by U.S. military/civic action teams and AID.

Not all parks in Costa Rica are government-owned. Some are managed privately, and cost as much as $75 a day to enjoy. This privatization of nature worries some Costa Rican environmentalists, who are also concerned about the explosion of an ecotourism industry largely controlled by foreigners. In the late 1980s there was a 50 percent increase in businesses catering to such avocations as bird watching and white-water rafting. The government, which has encouraged these new entrepreneurs, has begun to see the environment in terms of its ability to generate foreign exchange from international tourists.

Outstanding steps in environmental protection have distinguished Costa Rica over the past 15 years, notably the establishment of national parks and forest reserves. Yet at the same time, the country's ecology is being seriously undermined by rapid deforestation, extensive soil erosion, inappropriate land use, indiscriminate pesticide use, urban sprawl, and uncontrolled dumping of industrial wastes. Environmental organizations and experts abound in Costa Rica. Their recommendations and initiatives, however, often conflict with the country's model of economic development, whose extensive agroexport production depends on cheap land and labor.

One encouraging sign is the emergence of community environmental initiatives. Examples include the Guapiles neighborhood association's concern with deforestation, the struggle by the Desamparados community to stop coffee-processing plants from dumping wastes in nearby rivers, and the growing interest among peasant farmers in organic vegetable production. An ever present pitfall for all grassroots initiatives, however, is cooptation by the government or international institutions. The militancy and effectiveness of a leading environmental organization, ASCONA, was severely undermined by its association with PLN and AID, for example.[42]

Chapter 5

Foreign Influence

U.S. Foreign Policy

Costa Rica, a longtime ally of the United States, received special attention from Washington during the 1980s as a result of U.S. preoccupation with Nicaragua. In marked contrast to its destablization campaign against the Sandinista government, Washington launched an expensive stabilization effort in Costa Rica, which was promoted as a showcase of capitalist and democratic development. In return for U.S. economic aid, Costa Rica acceded to covert U.S. initiatives to establish a southern contra front. Tensions arose in the mid-1980s when Costa Rica began to resist U.S. attempts to involve it further in the contra war. The independence shown by President Arias in helping set the regional peace accords in motion was also a cause of tension in U.S.-Costa Rica relations. While generally a firm ally, Costa Rica also has liberal streak that Washington has not appreciated.

In 1955 U.S. Ambassador Robert Woodward reported to the State Department that Costa Rica's security forces "are handicapped in arresting communists because of the protection afforded the individual in the Costa Rican Constitution." But he noted that the "application of limited force" was possible if the United States provided Costa Rica with adequate intelligence and helped convince the public that "communism constituted a present menace." Furthermore, Woodward suggested that the public be "conditioned" to "the use of force by the authorities" by means of "a strong propaganda campaign."[1]

Through the years, U.S. government officials in Costa Rica have criticized aspects of Costa Rican government as being "socialistic." Costa Rica's early support for the Sandinistas, and the principled defense of revolutionary Nicaragua offered by José Figueres also irked Washington, as did the independence shown by President Arias in the regional peace process.

While the Costa Rican government has often shown more independence than Washington would like, it has proved a reliable U.S. ally
in the region on many occasions. President Figueres, for example, opened
the door to American Institute for Free Labor Development (AIFLD)
labor operations within the country and backed the Bay of Pigs invasion
of Cuba. Receiving some funding, Figueres even collaborated with
moderates within the CIA, but by the mid-1960s began expressing serious
reservations about U.S. foreign policy in Latin America.

Although Costa Rica has always provided a friendly climate for U.S.
investment and settlement, it was not until after 1982 that it began receiving substantial monetary rewards from Uncle Sam. These financial
benefits accrued in return for Costa Rica's cooperation with the U.S. anti-
Sandinista campaign. Costa Rica reluctantly allowed its territory to be
used to mount the contras' southern front, and the country's media became a mouthpiece for U.S. anti-Sandinista propaganda. In violation of
its own stated commitment to peace and neutrality, the Costa Rican
government also permitted the United States to bolster the capabilities
of the country's police forces.

The foreign policy of the Reagan administration and the peace initiatives of President Arias represented tactical differences in their attempts
to modify the Nicaraguan revolution. While Reagan was still holding firm
to the military option, Arias, with support from congressional Democrats
and other U.S. foreign-policy tacticians, recognized the futility of the contra war and advocated a negotiated settlement based on the full
democratization of Nicaragua.

The Arias peace initiatives did help to undermine the contras and
abate the war. But the Nicaraguan government and other observers of the
peace process came to question the sincerity of Arias' commitment to
regional peace and democracy given his practice of singling out Nicaragua
as the main violator of the accords. While disparities in strategy continued
to exist between the foreign-policy approaches of the U.S. and the Costa
Rican governments, President Arias consistently echoed the rhetoric in
Washington about Nicaragua being the main threat to democracy in the
region. He repeatedly referred to the military-controlled governments of
Honduras, Guatemala, and El Salvador as democracies while labeling
Nicaragua a Marxist dictatorship. Following President Arias' trip to
Washington in April 1989, the White House called Arias a very valuable
ally to whom the administration looked for leadership "as we try to apply
diplomatic pressure to Nicaragua to live up to its promises."

Washington's foreign policy in regard to Costa Rica cannot be
separated from its efforts to destabilize Nicaragua. While this anti-San-

dinista policy caused some inconveniences for Costa Rica, such as societal disruption and deceptions associated with the contra presence, it also proved to be the salvation of an economy on the edge of bankruptcy. The less than compliant position of Arias did lead to cutbacks and delays in U.S. aid designed to express U.S. displeasure. But AID noted in its 1989 congressional presentation: "Costa Rica will continue to require significant economic assistance over the next few years to avoid deterioration of living standards....The social and political risks of such a decline are contrary to U.S. interests in the region."[2]

Costa Ricans continue to be receptive to U.S. influence, especially when it means dollars flowing into the economy. But accelerated U.S. intervention in the country's internal affairs, such as the shaping of Costa Rica's economic and foreign policies, grated on the sensibilities of many Costa Ricans. A symbol of the deepening U.S. presence and influence is one that few have missed: the construction of an imposing, new fortress-like embassy that cost $11 million and houses 225 employees. Blocks away is an equally commanding new structure that contains the AID complex of offices. Some find this concrete demonstration of U.S. commitment to the country reassuring while others see the buildings to be self-indulgent manifestations of U.S. imperial might.

By the late 1980s U.S. foreign policy attention was shifting away from Central America. Although Washington's geopolitical concerns in the region diminished, it continued to push forward its agenda of conservative economic reform and free trade in the early 1990s. It expressed its pleasure both with new austerity measures that cut back social services and reduced the public-sector's payroll and with the President Calderón's commitment to promote private-sector interests, particularly those of U.S. traders and investors.

U.S. Trade and Investment

To the first-time visitor, the extent of U.S. influence in Costa Rica is startling. Menus in the classier restaurants are commonly bilingual, U.S. brand-name products are readily available, and there is a large U.S. community. Sale signs for choice houses and property are frequently only in English. To an extent not seen elsewhere in Central America, Costa Rica has become Americanized – in cultural values, style of dress, consumption patterns, and even political ideology. To a large degree, the dominance of U.S. trade and investment is responsible for this saturation of U.S. culture and values. But there is also an active identification on the part of Costa Rican society with anything and everything made in the USA.

Trade with the United States dwarfs commercial relations with other countries. About 65 percent of the country's exports (mostly coffee, bananas, cacao, and beef) are sold in the United States and about 45 percent of its imports (chemicals, industrial raw materials, consumer goods, vehicles, machinery, and grains) come from the United States.[3] Foreign investment pervades the economy, close to 60 percent of which is from the United States.[4]

Some 300 U.S. firms do business in Costa Rica, accounting for $550 million worth of investment according to the U.S. embassy.[5] Over one-third of these transnational corporations (TNCs) are in the manufacturing sector. The top five U.S. pharmaceutical corporations have operations in Costa Rica. Many TNCs take advantage of the country's cheap labor to assemble products as diverse as nuclear gauges, golf carts, yachts, and bird cages. Movie Star, Inc. produces underpants for export, Lovable manufactures a full line of women's lingerie, and Consolidated Foods assembles bras. Costa Rica also has several clothing manufacturers that subcontract assembly work with large U.S. clothing companies. Over 20 TNCs either manufacture or distribute chemicals (mostly pesticides and fertilizers). Seven of the top 20 TNC food processors produce for the nation's internal market. Colgate-Palmolive markets toothpaste and also manufactures candy, chocolates, and crackers through its subsidiary Pozuelo.

An impressive array of business equipment corporations, including IBM, Honeywell, Burroughs, ITT, and Xerox, market their products within the country. Five of the top eight accounting firms have offices, primarily to tend to the books of the other TNCs; and the top two U.S. banks—Citicorp and BankAmerica—serve the TNCs active in the country. Also in the service sector are McDonald's, Kentucky Fried Chicken, and Pizza Hut.

All three banana companies—Castle & Cooke, United Brands, and RJ Reynolds—have agribusiness operations, although United Brands pulled out of its banana investments in 1984 while retaining its palm oil investment. IU International has interests in sugar production, while Hershey and IC Industries are involved in the cocoa industry. Eight U.S. companies, including American Flower and Foliage, Inc., dominate the ornamental flowers and plants business.[6]

On several occasions, the U.S. embassy has used its economic-aid package as leverage to ensure better treatment of U.S. investors. One case in the late 1980s involved a U.S. contractor named Jack Parker who was suing the Costa Rican government for a breach of contract. Senator Jesse Helms took up his case and eventually the U.S. embassy threatened to freeze aid if the case was not settled favorably. Reacting to this interference, the government's Public Works Minister charged that Costa Rica was being treated like a banana republic.

Tico businessmen express deepening resentment at their government's favored treatment of U.S. investors. Special incentives – including tax credit certificates and exemptions from import and export duties – are available to U.S. investors and oftentimes not offered to local investors.

Another group selected for special treatment is the large community of foreign settlers who qualify for pensioner status in Costa Rica. To qualify for this special status (or an associated one called *rentista*) a foreigner has to receive $600 to $1,000 monthly from sources outside the country. This person then has the right to import (duty-free) a car, electronic items, and other household goods that are prohibitively expensive for Costa Ricans due to steep import taxes. The country's relatively advanced economic state and the government's efforts to attract foreigners have resulted in an extensive expatriate community in Costa Rica. Some 7,000 heads of households have been granted the special resident status, although many more foreigners live in Costa Rica as tourists, leaving the country every 90 days to renew their visas. The pensioners have their own association which has successfully fought off recent government attempts to chip away at their benefits in a effort to create more government revenue. About one-third of the pensioners are retired U.S. citizens while the balance are Chinese, European, and Canadian.

The 1970s and early 1980s were lean years in Costa Rica both for tourism and for foreigners seeking residency in Costa Rica. However, the international attention focused on Costa Rica as a result of Arias' Nobel Peace Prize and the government's own efforts to promote itself as an "escape to paradise" opened the doors to a new stream of foreigners seeking a peaceful tropical nirvana.

Foreigners are not only enjoying the beauty of Costa Rica, they are also buying and fencing it. In many areas, land prices have soared as foreigners have purchased choice sections of real estate. The English-language *Tico Times* runs several pages of ads for beachfront estates, plantations, and mountain hideaways. The American Realty Company entices the prospective buyer to "own your own plantation" or acquire over 2,000 acres of "rolling farmland for cattle and citrus." According to Terry Ennis, a realtor and director of the Pensioners Association, over 60 percent of Pacific coast beachfront property is now in the hands of foreigners.[7]

Because land speculation is common among foreign buyers, U.S. landowners have become the target of *precaristas*, the landless peasants who squat on uncultivated land. In several cases, the *precaristas* asserted that these foreign owners were using their land as transshipment points for drugs and were themselves involved in drug trafficking. One large landowner thus implicated was John Hull, a CIA functionary who helped organize the contras' southern front.

U.S. Economic Aid

Spread across a block of land on the outskirts of San José, the mammoth new Agency for International Development (AID) headquarters is surrounded by the luxury homes of the country's nouveau riche. One *Tico Times* reporter described the complex as "a monument to what some Costa Ricans are calling the parallel state." The $10 million building, christened "an appropriate capitol building for the parallel state," is the center for the U.S. government's efforts to stabilize and privatize the Costa Rican economy.[8] Like the nearby embassy, the AID headquarters is designed as a fortress with a rooftop heliport, emergency exits, and steel-reinforced concrete walls said to be tank-proof and unscalable.[9]

The term "parallel state" became part of the common political vocabulary in 1988 when a close adviser to President Arias, economist John Biehl, charged that AID was creating an infrastructure of private-sector institutions designed to undermine corresponding public ministries and agencies. The media and business elite were indignant, and the adviser was quickly removed from government. But the term "parallel state" stuck, and for many Costa Ricans remains the most apt description of AID operations.

The U.S. economic-assistance program to Costa Rica began in 1946 but it was not until the early 1980s that the country became a major recipient. In 1978 President Carter was considering removing Costa Rica from the list of AID beneficiaries because of the country's relatively high per capita income.[10] Instead, the level of aid was dramatically increased beginning in the early 1980s. From 1982-1990 Costa Rica received over $1.1 billion from AID.

The floodgates of economic assistance opened because of Costa Rica's newly acquired strategic importance as the southern neighbor of revolutionary Nicaragua. Costa Rica's rising political star coincided with its rapidly deteriorating economic fortunes. Just as Washington was developing a policy of containment and counterrevolution for Central America, Costa Rica was showing signs of economic collapse. In 1981 the country had stopped payment on its foreign debt because the national treasury was empty.

The focus of U.S. aid has been economic stabilization. Very little of the funds pumped into the country have been from AID's Development Assistance budget. Instead, virtually all the aid has come in the form of balance-of-payments support (either through the Economic Support Fund, ESF, or PL480 Title I food-aid program), designed to improve the country's foreign-exchange reserves while giving the government a flexible source of local revenue.[11] In addition to a small amount of Development Assistance, the U.S. economic-aid package includes a Peace Corps presence, a large scholarship program, and various credit and insurance arrangements sponsored by the Departments of Commerce, Agriculture, and Treasury.

Balance-of-payments support is the main thrust of AID's economic-stabilization plan for Costa Rica. An entire other level of U.S. strategy comes into play, however, with the use of the local currency created by all the U.S. dollars and food pumped into the domestic economy. For the most part, AID has directed these funds into two interrelated strategies of economic development: private-sector support and the promotion of nontraditional exports. It is mainly here, in the allocation of these local-currency funds, where the so-called "parallel state" has emerged.

Assisting the Private Sector

Although private-sector support has long been an element in AID's development philosophy, the Reagan administration converted it into the common denominator of the agency's development programs. In Costa Rica, this thrust took two directions: 1) a drive to privatize many public corporations and agencies, and 2) a multifaceted plan to bolster the country's business elite. Both phases of this private-support strategy have received vigorous support by the country's major media, the business community itself, and leading elements within the country's two major political parties. AID monies have financed a public-relations campaign that promotes the politics of private-sector support. The ubiquitous slogan of this campaign, which parallels similar campaigns throughout the region, equates democracy with unrestricted capitalism.

The privatization strategy garnered widespread public sympathy for its targeting of bureaucratic inefficiency and corruption prevalent in many government institutions. One target, CODESA, is a white elephant of a development corporation that just about everybody agrees should die. But privatization tentacles have also made gestures toward the electric company, and have even threatened to engulf the National Production Corporation (CNP), the institution responsible for protecting the interests of grain producers and low-income consumers. Asked why AID has not demanded that all government corporations be fully privatized, Neil Billig, the director of the agency's Private Sector Office confided, "We're already twisting the government's arm as hard as we can....We can't do it all, some are sacred cows."[12] AID's Private Sector Office has recognized that it must tread carefully in its privatization drive. It has adopted what it calls a "less inflammatory" and "low profile approach to further privatization."[13]

Closely associated with the privatization drive is an AID-backed plan to promote private banking in Costa Rica. According to AID, the government's banking structure is inefficient and tainted by politics. Furthermore, its control of most of the country's financial resources violates the principles of free enterprise. As a condition for continued economic assistance, AID obligated the Costa Rican government to allow private banks to benefit from international lines of credit from foreign donors like AID and to permit those banks to accept individual deposits – both previously prohibited under the country's system of nationalized banking.

The result was a proliferation of private financial institutions, a surplus of credit at these banks, and a substantial tightening of credit available to poor and working people through the government's financial system. As Ottón Solís, the country's former Planning Minister (who resigned as a result of AID's success in undermining the country's nationalized banking system), chided, "One of the corollaries of democracy is the avoidance of the concentration of wealth, which is what the national banking system has helped this country to do. It is, in fact, a fundamental mode of being in this society."[14]

Ironically, AID's rush to support private banking with economic-aid funds has resulted in a highly dependent and subsidized sector. Over 40 percent of the assets held by private banks come from AID credit lines.[15] Thus, like the public-sector institutions with which it is now competing, private finance is underwritten with public funds. AID acknowledged that the credit lines it offered the banks actually permitted them to provide subsidized loans to the business community.

According to Solís, this subsidized support for private banking contradicts the private-enterprise and free-market standards proclaimed by AID and the advocates of conservative economic policies. At the same time credit for small farmers and individual consumers can only be obtained at prohibitively high market rates (often over 30 percent). Because of the zeal shown by AID and other foreign donors in supporting private finance in Costa Rica, the banks are flooded with cheap money for which they cannot find enough outlets. The local private sector is still not ready to risk the quantity of new investment needed to pull the economy out of its slump — despite the ready supply of subsidized credit.

The other part of AID's private-sector support effort has been the shoring up of business associations and the offering of incentives and subsidies to private investment. It is AID's contention that private-sector institutions need to take a more prominent role in the formation of national economic policy and in the promotion of investment in Costa Rica. Given the lack of a preexisting Costa Rican business organization capable of assuming this role, AID created the Costa Rican Coalition for Development Initiatives (CINDE), which AID has infused with tens of millions of dollars since 1983.

To critics of AID, CINDE represents the paramount example of the "parallel state." Rather than channeling agricultural assistance, investment promotion, credit, and industrial development funds through government institutions, AID chose to hatch a new organization to receive its grants. The government has an export-promotion agency called CENPRO, whose effectiveness has been limited by a small budget and low salaries. Rather than working to improve CENPRO, AID devised a component of CINDE, known as the Investment Promotion Program (PIE), to undertake the same functions. The difference is that PIE has a multi-million dollar budget and can attract the best talent with salary levels comparable to the United States. PIE, for example, spends $1 million annually simply to operate four foreign promotional offices (three in the United States and one in Paris).

Other instances of this "parallel state" include the Private Agricultural and Agroindustrial Council (CAAP), which, like PIE, budded as a branch of CINDE. The activities of CAAP parallel those of the Ministry of Agriculture, but are exclusively oriented to the promotion of agroexport production. A revealing display of teamwork was exhibited when CAAP rallied the private-sector lobby to push through the National Assembly's authorization of the controversial EARTH (Agricultural School for the Humid Tropics), yet another AID-created parallel institution programmed to serve only 400 students.

AID's plan to spend $118 million to establish EARTH sparked vociferous opposition among the academic community. Students, professors, and a university rector joined in the protest, arguing that the school was not necessary and contributed to the undermining of the government's higher education system. While the government's own budget was being squeezed by economic policies fostered by AID, the U.S. government was spending over a hundred million dollars to build a school that most Costa Ricans thought unnecessary. Resentment toward EARTH also represented a more general concern about the rise of private schools and universities, some of which also received AID funds.

Other prominent examples of parallel institutions include the AID-sponsored Costa Rica Highway and Road Association (which competes with the Ministry of Public Works and Transport) and the Private Investment Corporation (which assumes many of the functions of CODESA). In addition, AID has given birth to an array of research, educational, and community development organizations that together form part of an AID-controlled private infrastructure. One such institution is the Center for Political-Administration Training (CIAPA), a rightwing think tank which is a center for attacks on the regional peace plan and the government's social-welfare policies. This ideological support network provides a powerful base for the neoliberal and export-oriented strategies promoted by AID, while undermining the social structure established by the reformist state in Costa Rica.

Addressing the issue of the "parallel state," John Biehl observed, "They ended up with this fiction: When something is financed with Costa Rican taxpayers' money, it's public sector and inefficient. When the same thing is financed by U.S. taxpayers' money, it's private sector and efficient." This sardonic remark was offered about the same time that an AID Inspector General report highlighted the corrupt and often ineffective nature of AID-financed programs in Costa Rica. The report lambasted CINDE for lacking the managerial capacity to administer the large AID grants and for its inability to produce tangible results as AID money for privatization was siphoned off through loans to the directors of CINDE and other AID projects. According to the audit report, "This organization [CINDE] has done little to promote development, but appears to have been utilized by a few prominent Costa Ricans to advance their own personal and political interests, and as a temporary resting place or springboard for aspiring politicians." Even the Central America Peace Scholarship (CAPS) program administered by AID was abused, with the sons, daughters, and relatives of some of the country's most influential families receiving scholarships targeted for the poor.[16]

In 1988 the U.S. embassy faced opposition to the large injection of U.S. economic aid into the country from an unlikely source. Over half the 170 Peace Corps volunteers based in the country signed a petition objecting to the planned increase of the Peace Corps contingent to 225 volunteers.[17] Those signing the petition complained that there was already a surplus of Peace Corps staff in the country and that many communities felt they were being inundated by volunteers who, in some cases, displaced Costa Rican government workers. The petition said: "It strikes us as strange that this decision to increase volunteer placement in Central America was not based on requests by community groups or Peace Corps program managers, but rather was originated and decided upon in Washington. This points to political considerations behind the decision."[18]

The results are not yet in on the full success or failure of AID's intervention in Costa Rica. AID can point to a tripling of nontraditional exports, but the development impact of this achievement is undercut by two factors: 1) most of the investment in nontraditional export production is in the hands of U.S. investors who repatriate their profits, and 2) nontraditional exports from the industrial sector are almost entirely assembly-type manufactured goods which provide little direct investment or value-added components to the Costa Rican economy. Although the injection of large sums of U.S. economic aid have indeed allowed Costa Rica to escape the clutches of financial bankruptcy, there is much uncertainty about whether the structural adjustments imposed by AID and other international institutions have equipped the country with the economic base and direction it needs for long-term stability.

Uncertain Future

Since the mid-1980s the level of aid received by Costa Rica has been declining. In 1985, Monge's last year in office, the country received over $230 million. By the late 1980s the country could only count on $118 million in U.S. aid. Economic aid was down to $76 million in 1990 and $50 million in 1991, with only $28 million requested for 1992.

Politics and economics have both figured into this pattern of decreasing U.S. aid. On the political side, the need to reward Costa Rica with "quid pro quo" aid decreased as the U.S. military campaign against Nicaragua was scaled down. Washington also found that it was not getting the "quid" for its "quo" from the Arias government. By calling off the special deals that allowed the United States to use Costa Rica as the "southern front," President Arias was punished with decreasing commitments of U.S. aid. Republican wrath with Arias has been balanced, at least in part, by warm relations with the Democrats in Congress. But this alliance with the Democrats supporting the regional peace plan has not paid off in the economic dividends expected by Arias. Neither did his political initiatives pay off in terms of increased European aid.

The political tension between the Arias government and the White House certainly was a factor in aid cutbacks in the late 1980s. But AID never promised Costa Rica a future bankrolled by economic aid. After more than a billion dollars in direct economic aid in addition to an infusion of multilateral assistance, the Costa Rican economy has emerged from its earlier crisis. In AID's terms, it has been stabilized, making it harder to justify the authorization of large sums of ESF money.

By 1990 it became more difficult to justify large chunks of Development Assistance to this middle-income country, especially when the foreign-aid budget was falling. The installation of a new government in Panama in December 1989 and the Sandinistas' electoral defeat two months later also meant that strategic importance of Costa Rica had diminished. The dramatic drop in economic aid has not discouraged AID from using its aid package as leverage for conservative policy reforms. The agency says it will use its 1992 aid to support policy dialogue in three strategic areas: trade and investment, public-sector restructuring, and natural resources management.

U.S. Military Aid

After a lapse of 14 years Washington began supplying military aid and training to Costa Rica in 1981. At that time, former Ambassador to the United Nations Jeane Kirkpatrick insisted that Costa Rica accept "security assistance" as a condition for increased economic aid. Both U.S. and Costa Rican officials have denied that U.S. military aid undermines the country's professed commitment to neutrality and demilitarization. Through the International Military Education and Training (IMET) and Military Assistance Program (MAP), over $30 million in aid and $1 million in training was provided to the Civil and Rural Guards between 1980 and 1988. Costa Rican forces have received such items as helicopters, jeeps, mortars, munitions, and a wide selection of high-powered rifles. Over 1200 members of Costa Rica's security forces have been trained locally by U.S. Mobile Training Teams (MTT) in addition to some 300 trained outside the country in Panama and at Fort Benning, Georgia.

Civic-action projects by U.S. National Guard and Army units have become an annual event in Costa Rica. In 1989 some 750 U.S. soldiers arrived to build bridges and roads in the isolated Osa Peninsula as part of a program that U.S. embassy dubbed "Roads for Peace." Besides road and bridge construction, U.S. military/civic action programs have also drilled wells, repaired school buildings, and provided medical assistance.

The programs have the dual purpose of generating goodwill towards the U.S. military and providing military engineer and medical units with valuable experience in tropical areas.

The U.S. Department of Defense lists four objectives of its security assistance to Costa Rica: 1) to assist in economic stabilization and recovery, 2) to modernize and professionalize the country's security forces, 3) to enable Costa Rica to maintain surveillance of its borders and protect its territorial sovereignty, and 4) to enable the security forces to respond to internal threats with discipline.[19]

With the sometimes halting cooperation of the Costa Rica government, Washington supported the southern front of the contra war along the country's northern border with Nicaragua. The corruption, intrigue, and depravity associated with that operation continues to plague U.S.-Costa Rica relations. A report on the 1984 La Penca bombing issued in late 1989 by the country's judicial authorities revealed the dirty underside of U.S. foreign-policy operations in the 1980s. The report blamed the bombing, which occurred at a contra camp in Nicaragua just across the Costa Rican border, on U.S. contra supporters, the CIA, and the FDN, which was the dominant contra group. Although targeting maverick contra leader Eden Pastora, the bombing killed three journalists attending a news conference and injured a dozen more, including Tony Avirgan. The report confirmed claims by Avirgan and Martha Honey that the CIA had formed a unit called the "Babies" within Costa Rica's Directorate of Intelligence and Security that took orders directly from the CIA. It also recommended that U.S. rancher/CIA operative John Hull and CIA operative Felipe Vidal be charged with first-degree murder for the bombing.

Other Foreign Interests

The United States dominates trade, investment, and foreign-aid programs in Costa Rica, but the country also maintains close ties with Taiwan, West Germany, and Israel. In the period 1975-1985 trade with the European Economic Community (EEC) remained stable. About 20 percent of Costa Rica's exports (mainly coffee and bananas) go to the EEC and about 16 percent of its imports come from EEC countries. At the same time, trade with Japan dipped slightly and trade with other Latin American countries suffered a sharp decline. Paralleling U.S. aid programs, EEC economic aid to Costa Rica increased sharply in the 1980s but still is insignificant when compared with the type and quantity of U.S. aid. While most U.S. aid comes in the form of balance-of-payments support, virtually all of the some $40 million in EEC assistance during the 1980s has been in the form of technical assistance and credit.

West Germany is Costa Rica's main trading partner within the EEC. The West German group most active in Costa Rica is the Ebert Foundation, which finances the PLN's training courses for community, cooperative, and political leaders. The conservative Konrad Adenauer Foundation finances the John XXIII Social School for *solidarismo* organizing. (See Labor)

In 1982 relations between Israel and Costa Rica improved dramatically with the advent of the Monge administration. The following year, Israel provided security and intelligence training for the country's police forces and initiated exchange·and agricultural-assistance programs. As one of the few countries to move its embassy (President Monge's former workplace) from Tel Aviv to Jerusalem, Costa Rica gained favor with the Israelis.

Ties with Taiwan

Another unlikely international ally, Taiwan for years has courted the Costa Rican police and its political elite with scholarships for instruction in psychological operations and counterinsurgency. Lately, a considerable economic aspect to this alliance has developed, with Taiwan sharply increasing both its aid to and investment in Costa Rica since 1987. Although Panama, El Salvador, Honduras, and Guatemala also maintain close relations with the Asian island, Costa Rica seems to be the primary beneficiary of Taiwan's new attentions.

While most of the upgrading of the Costa Rican security forces is the result of U.S. programs, a significant, but undisclosed, amount comes from Taiwan. When repressing peasant demonstrations, the Civil Guard is likely to be using riot gear and carrying M-16s that come by way of Taiwan. It is, however, in the area of ideological and counterinsurgency training where Taiwan has most influenced the country's security forces. Hundreds of Costa Rican ministers, politicians, and police officers have received training at the Fu Hsing Kang College in Taiwan, which offers a two-month long "Higher Course in Political Warfare."[20] Since 1974 Costa Ricans have attended more than 80 political warfare courses.

According to a report by Joel Millman of the Institute of Current World Affairs in New Hampshire, diplomas from the Fu Hsing Kang College are displayed on the walls of many government officials. Most officers of the Civil Guard have attended the course, and graduates can also be found directing the private security forces of such companies as Del Monte. When asked about the value of the political warfare course, Julio

Morales, vice president of Costa Rica's Fu Hsing Kang alumni club explained: "Suppose Rambo was fighting for us and he was killing Sandinistas. All of sudden he hears a voice over a loudspeaker: 'Rambo, all your leaders are gone. Costa Rica has fallen, the President is in Miami. Give up, Rambo.' If he hadn't taken the political warfare course he would not know that this is a typical communist trick, and he would surrender."

In 1988 Taiwan gave Costa Rica a $55 million loan, apparently as part of its major initiative to establish Taiwan assembly plants in the country's export-processing zones (EPZs). Taiwanese investors plan to establish some two dozen labor-intensive assembly plants that will export to the United States under the duty-free provisions of the Caribbean Basin Initiative. In addition, these companies will benefit from the new series of incentives, subsidies, and tax exemptions established by Costa Rica under an export-promotion plan sponsored by AID. Yet another element of Taiwan's increasing interest in Costa Rica is its offer to finance the purchase of 40 percent of the country's foreign debt owed to private commercial banks. In exchange, Taiwan would probably be given special trading and investment privileges, including an exclusive tuna fishing agreement for the rich waters around Coco Island.

The economic initiatives of Taiwan are not unrelated to its military and ideological foreign-policy objectives. It views Central America as a solid supporter at a time when most countries have cut diplomatic ties with the island nation. Taiwan's commercial attaché in San José says the EPZs are "about fighting communism and building democracy. We warn our allies that a trade mission from the Communists is the first step toward a break in relations. They can't allow the Peoples Republic of China in and keep our friendship."[21]

Reference Notes

Introduction

1. J.D. Trejos and M.L. Elisalde, "Costa Rica: La Distribución del Ingreso y el Acceso a los Programas de Carácter Social," (San José: Instituto de Investigaciones Económicas, Universidad de Costa Rica, 1985), p.42.
2. Samuel Z. Stone, *La Dinastía de los Conquistadores: La Crisis del Poder en la Costa Rica Contemporanea* (San José: Editorial Universitaria, 1975).
3. Leonardo Garnier, "Crisis, Desarrollo, y Democracia en Costa Rica," in *Costa Rica: Crisis y Desafíos* (San José: Departamento Ecuménico de Investigaciones/Centro de Estudios para la Acción Social-CEPAS, 1987), p.41.

Chapter One

1. See Garnier, op.cit., and Manuel Rojas Bolaños, "Ocho Tesis sobre la Realidad Nacional," in *Costa Rica: Crisis y Desafíos*, op.cit.; Diego Palma, "El Estado y la Desmovilización en Costa Rica," *Estudios Sociales Centroamericanos*, No.27, 1980.
2. Excerpts of the Diego Palma essay are included in *The Costa Rica Reader*, Marc Edelman and Joanne Kenen, eds. (New York: Grove Weidenfield, 1989).
3. The author acknowledges that this analysis comes largely from an essay by Leonardo Garnier, "Crisis, Desarrollo, y Democracia en Costa Rica" in *Costa Rica: Crisis y Desafíos*, op.cit., pp.29-45. Also see an essay by Bolaños in the same volume, op.cit.
4. Manuel Rojas Bolaños and Carlos Sojo Obando, "A la Tercera Va la Vencida," *Pensamiento Propio*, March 1990.
5. *Latin American Regional Reports Mexico and Central America*, March 29, 1990.
6. *Costa Rica: Balance de la Situación* (CEPAS), January-March 1990, pp.9-11.
7. Daniel García, "Costa Rica: La Subsidaria Política Exterior," *Pensamiento Propio*, March 1990.
8. *Costa Rica: Balance de la Situación*, January-March 1990.
9. For a valuable summary of Costa Rica's role in the Esquipulas Peace Accords, see Carlos Sojo Obando, *Juez y Parte: Costa Rica en Esquipulas* (San José: Centro de Estudios para la Acción Social, 1990).
10. John McPhaul, "Debate Rages on Regional Parliament," *Miami Herald*, May 25, 1989.
11. Pax Christi International, *Human Rights in Central America*, 1988.
12. CODEHUCA, *Informe Anual 1987: Situación de Derechos Humanos en Centroamérica*.

Chapter Two

1. Interview with Vice Minister of Foreign Relations Luis Guillermo Solís, quoted in the unpublished report, "Narcotics War: Going for the Gold" by Joel Millman (Institute of Current World Affairs), March 8, 1988.

2. The main source for this section is an excellent article by Jean Hopfensperger, "Costa Rica: Seeds of Terror," *The Progressive*, September 1986.

3. Ibid.

Chapter Three

1. Juan Manuel Villasuso Etomba, "Evolución de la Crisis Económica en Costa Rica y su Impacto sobre la Distribución del Ingreso," in *Costa Rica Hoy: La Crisis y sus Perspectivas* (San José: Editorial UNED, 1983), excerpted in *The Costa Rica Reader*, op.cit.

2. *Latin American Weekly Report*, March 15, 1990.

3. Charles D. Ameringer, *Democracy in Costa Rica* (New York: Praeger, 1982), p.94.

4. Andrew Redding, "Costa Rica: Democratic Model in Jeopardy," *World Policy Journal*, Spring 1986.

5. Costa Rica Ministry of Information, *Comunicación para la Democracia*, 1984.

6. This critique is found in "Privatización: Un Nuevo Reto para los Trabajadores" in *Panorama Sindical* (CEPAS), November 1987; and "La Privatización de lo Público" in *Costa Rica: Balance de la Situación*, August-October 1988.

7. Sources for this section on export crops included: Wilmer Murillo, "Transnacionales Aumentan su Poder Económico en Costa Rica," *La República*, October 28, 1988; U.S. Department of Agriculture, *Costa Rica Agricultural Situation Annual 1988* (Foreign Agricultural Service).

8. National Production Council, "Compendios Estadísticos Anuales," 1985-1988; *Costa Rica: Balance de la Situación*, April-May 1989.

9. *Costa Rica: Balance de la Situación*, January-March 1990, p.22.

10. Abelardo Morales, "Democracia Rural Cede Terreno al Latifundio," *Aportes* (Editorial Aportes para la Educación), May-June 1984.

11. Beatriz M. Villareal, *Precarismo Rural en Costa Rica* (San José: Editorial Papiro, 1983), p.25.

12. Mitchell A. Seligson, *Peasants of Costa Rica and the Development of Agrarian Capitalism* (Madison: University of Wisconsin, 1980), p.165.

13. *Rumbo*, July 1989.

14. *Costa Rica: Balance de la Situación*, April-May 1989.

15. Bruce W. Fraser, "Costa Rica Woos Foreign Investors," *Christian Science Monitor*, April 13, 1989.

Chapter Four

1. "El Sector Urbano Común," in *Costa Rica: Balance de la Situación*, November-December 1988.

2. Lezak Shallat, "Los Agricultores Se Enfrentan al Gobierno," *Pensamiento Propio*, September 1988.

3. Bolaños, "Ocho Tesis sobre la Realidad Nacional," op.cit., p.26.

4. "El Movimiento Sindical en Cifras," in *Panorama Sindical*, April 1988.

5. U.S. Department of Labor, *Foreign Labor Trends: Costa Rica 1987-1988*.

6. *Costa Rica: Balance de la Situación*, January-March 1990, p.17.

7. Curtin Winsor, Jr., "The Solidarista Movement: Labor Economics for Democracy," *The Washington Quarterly*, Fall 1986.

8. Interview with Patricia Matamoros, ACORDE, March 31, 1989.

9. Lezak Shallat, "Solidarismo Invades Last Union Stronghold," *The Tico Times*, August 7, 1987.

10. Winsor, op.cit.

11. *The Costa Rica Reader*, op.cit.

12. Ibid.; *Inforpress Centroamericano*, March 9, 1987.

13. Two valuable articles on media manipulation in Costa Rica are: "The Continuing War: Media Manipulation in Costa Rica" by Howard Friel and Michell Joffroy in *Covert Action Information Bulletin*, Summer 1986; and "Back in Control" by Jacqueline Sharkey in *Common Cause Magazine*, September-October 1986.

14. For details, see: Jean Hopfensperger, "Costa Rica, Seeds of Terror," *The Progressive*, September 1986 and Jean Hopfensperger, "U.S. and Contras Find Ally in Costa Rica's Three Major Dailies," *Christian Science Monitor*, July 18, 1986.

15. Martha Honey, "Contra Coverage Paid for by the CIA: The Company Goes to Work in Central America," *Columbia Journalism Review*, March-April 1987. According to Morales, the eight journalists are each paid 30,000 *colones* monthly while the monthly salary of most Costa Rican journalists averages about 20,000 *colones*.

16. Communication with Martha Honey, July 1989.

17. Main sources for this section: World Health Organization, *World Health Statistics Annual 1988*; and "Caos Sanitario en el País" in *Costa Rica: Balance de la Situación*, August-October 1987.

18. Lynn M. Morgan, "Health Effects of the Costa Rican Economic Crisis" in *The Costa Rica Reader*, op.cit.

19. Ibid.

20. U.S. Agency for International Development, *Health Sector Policy Paper*, 1982; and ibid.

21. Richard Garfield, "Health and Development in Central America," *Journal of the American Medical Association*, No.254, 1985, pp.936-943.

22. Morgan, op.cit.

23. Much of this discussion of the history and social vision of the Catholic church is digested from: Andrés Opazo Bernales, *Costa Rica: La Iglesia Católica y el Orden Social* (San José: Departamento Ecuménico de Investigaciones, 1987).

24. Ibid.

25. *Directorio de Iglesias, Organizaciones, y Ministros del Movimiento Protestante: Costa Rica* (San José: PROLADES, 1986).

26. Ibid.

27. *World Christianity: Central America and the Caribbean*, Clifton L. Holland, ed. (Monrovia, CA: MARC/World Vision International, 1981).

28. *Rumbo*, July 1989.

29. Interview with Kris Merschrod, PACT, April 1988.

30. Emma Daly, "Child Abuse Increasing," *The Tico Times*, April 15, 1988.

31. Emma Daly, "Violence Against Women Increasing in Costa Rica," *The Tico Times*, April 8, 1988.

32. CEPAL, *Diagnóstico de la Situación de la Mujer Centroamericana*, 1988.

33. Cited in "Sterilization in Costa Rica," an article by Abigail Adams in *Links* (NCAHRN), Winter 1987.

34. *Central America Report*, September 1, 1989.

35. Carolyn Hall, *Costa Rica: A Geographical Interpretation in Historical Perspective* (Boulder: Westview Press, 1985), p.45.

36. Brian Houseal, Craig MacFarland, Guillermo Archibold, and Aurelio Chiari, "Indigenous Cultures and Protected Areas in Central America," *Cultural Survival Quarterly*, Vol.9, No.1, 1985.

37. William Vargas Mora, "Intereses Foraneos Contra Indígenas de Talamanca," *Aportes*, July 1988.

38. "Nicaraguan Refugees in Costa Rica," in *Mesoamerica*, June 1989.

39. Bill Weinberg, *War on the Land: The Politics of Ecology and the Ecology of Politics in Central America*, unpublished manuscript.

40. *La Nación*, May 25, 1987.

41. Alexander Bonilla D., *Situación Ambiental en Costa Rica* (ASCONA), no date.

42. *Aportes*, December 1988. ASCONA became defunct in 1989 after having simultaneously lost its volunteer basis and its AID funding.

Chapter Five

1. Noam Chomsky, *Necessary Illusions* (Boston: South End Press, 1989), pp.264-265.

2. U.S. Agency for International Development, *Congressional Presentation, FY1989*.

3. U.S. Embassy, "Business Fact Sheet," compiled June 1989.

4. Ibid.

5. The book value of U.S. investment is given at only $115 million by the U.S. Department of Commerce.

6. Most information on extent of U.S. corporate investment comes from: The Resource Center, "Compilation of Corporations," 1985.

7. Interview by Debra Preusch (Resource Center), March 1989.

8. Lezak Shallat, "AID and the Parallel State," in *The Costa Rica Reader*, op.cit.

9. Martha Honey, "Costa Rica: U.S. Imposes Its Ideology," *Los Angeles Times*, October 30, 1988.

10. Martha Honey, "Undermining a Friend: The Impact of Reagan/Bush Policies in Costa Rica," July 1989.

11. Both the ESF and Title I programs function as balance-of-payments support, either by injecting dollars directly into the national treasury (ESF) or shipping food commodities which would have otherwise required scarce dollars to purchase (Title I). When the coveted foreign exchange (ESF) or food (Title I) are then sold to the private sector on the local market, the government obtains a sum of local currency equal to the value of the two programs.

12. Interview by author with Neil Billig, U.S. Agency for International Development/Costa Rica, Private Sector Office, March 1989.

13. U.S. Agency for International Development/Costa Rica, Rica-Private Sector Office, "Three Year Strategy," January 25, 1988.

14. Interview by author with Ottón Solís, March 1989.

15. Ibid.

16. Abelardo Morales Gamboa, "Ricos y Famosos Se Benefician con AID," *Aportes*, March 1988.

17. In mid-1989, there were 215 Peace Corps volunteers assigned to Costa Rica.

18. Peter Brennan, "Peace Corps Volunteers Protest Expansion," *The Tico Times*, March 29, 1988.

19. U.S. Department of Defense, *Congressional Presentation for Security Assistance, FY1989*.

20. According to Joel Millman, official figures of the number of Costa Ricans who have received training in Taiwan are not revealed by either government, but estimates run from 200 to as many as 800.

21. Joel Millman, "Central America is Fertile Ground for Taiwan's Surplus," *Wall Street Journal*, July 1, 1988.

Statistics

Population

Population:	3,033,000 (1990)[1]
Urban Population:	50.3% (1988)[2]
Population Density:	154 per sq. mi.
Annual Growth Rate:	2.6% (1991)[1]
Literacy:	93.1%[1]
Ethnic Composition:[3]	
Black:	2%
Indian:	0.5%
Religion:	
Catholic:	84%
Protestant:	16%[4]

Health

Life Expectancy at Birth:	76.5 years (1990)[1]
Infant Mortality per 1,000 Live Births:	17.5 (1990)[5]

Economy

GDP:	$6,404 million (1988)[2]
Per Capita GDP:	$1,690 (1988)[1]
Income Distribution (1980):[6]	
Poorest 20% of Population:	4% of income
30% Below the Mean:	17% of income
30% Above the Mean:	30% of income
Richest 20%:	49% of income
Rural Population in Absolute Poverty:	40%[7]

(Absolute poverty is the inability to afford food providing minimum nutritional requirements.)

Land Distribution:[8]
1% of farms comprise 36% of farmland
46% of farms comprise 2% of farmland

External Public Debt:	
1970:	$134 million[9]
1990:	$2,985 million[10]

Trade Balance:
   Debt Servicing as % of Exports: -539.7 million (1990)[10]
   External Debt as % of GNP: 77.9% (1988)[1]
Property & Income Taxes as % of Current Revenues: 15.6% (1988)[2]
Labor Force by Sector (1985):[11]
   Agriculture: 27%
   Community Social & Personal Services: 25%
   Commerce: 19%
Unemployment: 5.5% (1987)[12]
Underemployment: 9.1% (1987)[12]
Top Agriculture Products: Coffee, Bananas, Cacao

U.S. Economic Aid[13]
(millions of dollars)

	1946-1979	1980-1988	1989	1990	1991*
Development Assistance	158.2	148.2	9.8	10.6	8.2
ESF	0	835.1	90.1	63.5	25.0
PL480	19.4	131.3	15.1	0.2	15.0
Peace Corps	15.3	19.7	3.5	2.2	1.9
Total	192.9	1,134.3	118.5	76.5	50.1

U.S. Military Aid[13]
(millions of dollars)

	1946-1979	1980-1988	1989	1990	1991*
MAP	0.9	30.4	0	0	0
FMS	5.0	0	0	0	0
IMET	0.9	1.3	0.2	0.2	0.2
Total	6.8	31.7	0.2	0.2	0.2

*Estimated

Sources:
1) U.S. Agency for International Development, Congressional Presentation FY1992;
2) Inter-American Development Bank, Economic and Social Progress in Latin America: 1989 Report; 3) Europa Year Book, 1987; 4) PROLADES, Directorio de Iglesias, Organizaciones, y Ministros del Movimiento Protestante: Costa Rica (San José: 1986); 5) Costa Rica Ministry of Development and Planning, 1991; 6) CEPAL Review, April 1984; 7) Tom Barry, Roots of Rebellion (Boston: South End Press, 1987); 8) CEPAL, La Agroindustria y el Sistema Alimentario Centroamericano, 1983; 9) World Bank, World Development Report 1988; 10) CEPAL, Preliminary Estimates, Notas sobre la Economía y el Desarrollo, December 1990; 11) Europa Year Book, 1988; 12) U.S. Department of Labor, Foreign Labor Trends: Costa Rica 1987-1988; 13) U.S. Agency for International Development, Office of Planning and Budgeting, U.S. Overseas Loans and Grants: Obligations and Loan Authorizations July 1, 1945-September 30, 1983; U.S. Agency for International Development, Office of Planning and Budgeting, U.S. Overseas Loans and Grants: Obligations and Loan Authorizations July 1, 1945-September 30, 1989; U.S. Agency for International Development, Fiscal Year 1992 Summary Tables.

Chronology

1821	Central American region declares its independence from Spain.
1822	Annexation to Mexico.
1823	Independence from Mexico as United Provinces of Central America.
	U.S. pronouncement of Monroe Doctrine.
1826	Outbreak of civil war.
1830	Morazán takes Guatemala City, becomes president of United Provinces of Central America.
1835	San José declared capital.
	Conservative Carillo takes power.
1838	Central American federation breaks into five states.
	Carillo declares himself president of Costa Rica for life.
1842	Carillo ousted by Morazán, who tries to re-establish federation.
	Morazán overthrown and executed.
1844	New Costa Rican constitution promulgated.
1849	Establishment of conservative government under Mora Porras.
1859	Mora resigns, Montealegre family takes power which it will hold for a decade.
	New constitution promulgated.
1860	Mora leads a failed invasion attempt and is executed.
1869	New constitution promulgated.
1870	Liberal government under Guardia.
1871	New liberal constitution promulgated.
	First railroad opens Atlantic coast to banana production.
1890	Inauguration of conservative government under Rodríguez.
	Formation of the Artisans Constitutional Club.
	Formation of the Catholic Union Party by Bishop Bernardo Augusto Thiel.
1894	Rodríguez's nominee Iglesias becomes president.
1901	Formation of the Workers League.
1902	Election of liberal Esquivel.
1906	Inconclusive election; Congress chooses liberal candidate González.
	Because it has been less involved in regional conflicts, Costa Rica begins to be seen as a natural mediator and home for exiled dissidents.
1910	Election of conservative Jiménez Oreamuno.
1913	Formation of the General Confederation of Workers (CGT).
1914	Inconclusive election; Congress chooses non-candidate González Flores.

1917	Tinoco seizes power in coup and abrogates constitution.
1918	U.S. President Wilson influences the governing of Costa Rica and encourages development of oil resources.
1919	Tinoco resigns; constitution of 1871 restored.
	CGT sparks formation of the Socialist Center.
1921	Latin American Mission begins its evangelizing campaigns.
1923	CGT dissolves to form Reformist Party.
1924	Jiménez Oreamuno elected for second term.
	Revision of penal code to outlaw most strikes.
1928	González elected.
1931	Formation of Communist Party (PC) under Mora Valverde.
1932	Formation of National Republican Party (PRN).
	Jiménez Oreamuno elected for third term.
1934	Massive banana worker strike led by PC.
	Formation of the Costa Rican Workers Confederation.
1936	PRN candidate Cortés elected.
1940	PRN candidate Calderón Guardia elected in landslide.
	Cortés forms Democratic Party (PD).
1941	New Labor Code recognizes right to strike; broad social-security program established.
	Figueres Ferrer denounces President Calderón in radio speech and is sent into exile.
1943	PC reorganized as Popular Vanguard Party (PVP).
1944	PRN-PVP coalition candidate Picado Michalski elected.
1945	Formation of the Rerum Novarum Costa Rican Workers Confederation (CCTRN).
1947	Formation of Democratic Renovation Party (PRD) by Carazo.
1948	
Feb.	Election won by Ulate Blanco of a coalition comprised of PD, Social Democratic Party (PSD), and National Unification Party (PUN). PRN wins majority in Congress, which annuls the presidential election results.
Mar.	Civil war breaks out; the 1948 "revolution."
	Figueres receives substantial U.S. support (and·later admits to CIA connections).
Apr.	Picado overthrown by forces led by Figueres.
May	Formation of the Junta of Second Republic, with Figueres acting as president.
Dec.	Picado supporters stage unsuccessful invasion attempt from Nicaragua.
1949	Ulate inaugurated as president.
	New constitution promulgated which abolishes army, franchises women, and outlaws PVP.
	Formation of the Socialist Action Party (PAS).
	Catholicism declared official religion.
	Banks nationalized.
1951	Formation of National Liberation Party (PLN) by Figueres.
1953	PLN candidate Figueres elected.
	Formation of Costa Rican General Workers Confederation (CGTC).

1955	Unsuccessful invasion attempts by exiles based in Nicaragua.
1958	PUN candidate Echandí Jiménez elected.
1961	Formation of the paramilitary Free Costa Rica Movement (MCRL).
1962	PLN candidate Orlich Bolmarich elected.
	Formation of Christian Democratic Party (PDC).
	Full relations broken with Cuba.
1963	Costa Rica joins the Central American Common Market (CACM).
1966	National Unification Coalition candidate Trejos Fernández elected.
1968	Archbishop of San José abstains from signing the Medellín document.
1969	Constitution of 1949 amended.
1970	PLN candidate Figueres elected.
	Anti-government protest over U.S. interest denounced by government as being provoked by "communist elements."
1971	Formation of Authentic Central Democratic Workers (CATD) after split with Costa Rican Confederation of Workers (CCTD).
1972	Formation of Costa Rican Workers Central (CTC).
1974	Use of the words "Marxist" and "Communist" banned during pre-election period by Supreme Electoral Tribunal.
	PLN candidate Oduber Quiros elected.
1975	Government purchase of uncultivated United Brands land; sexist use of women's bodies in commercial advertising banned.
	Trade relations with Cuba re-established.
	PVP returned to legal status.
1976	Splits in PLN and PUN.
	Formation of Calderonista Republican Party (PRC).
1977	Restoration of consular relations with Cuba.
	Indigenous Bill establishes right of Indians to land reserves.
1978	Formation of the Social Christian Unity Party (PSUC), a coalition of PRD, PRC, PDC, and PUP (Popular Unity Party), led by Calderón Fournier.
	Opposition Union candidate Carazo Odio elected; PVP-MRP gains three seats in legislative election.
1979	Support of the FSLN revolutionaries in Nicaragua.
	Formation of the Unitary Confederation of Workers (CUT).
1980	Formation of Costa Rican Solidarista Union (SURSUM).
1981	United States begins military aid and police training after 14-year lapse.
May	Parliamentary commission report on government involvement in arms trafficking to the FSLN.
	Consular relations with Cuba are broken.
Sep.	Moratorium on debt payments.
1982	PLN candidate Monge Alvarez elected.
	Government asks 17 Soviet diplomats to leave the country.
	Foreign Ministers of Costa Rica, El Salvador, and Honduras form the Central American Democratic Community.
1983	Contadora group meets for first time to develop dialogue and negotiation in Central America; parties to the peace accords include Costa Rica, El Salvador, Guatemala, Honduras, and Nicaragua.

Division in PVP; Mora leaves to form People's Party (PPC).

Unity coalition renamed Social Christian Unity (PUSC) under Calderón.

Formation of National Confederation of Workers (CNT) by AIFLD.

Presence of contras on Costa Rican territory increases tension with Nicaragua.

Foreign debt soars 40 percent to $4 billion over a seven-month period.

Israel begins security and intelligence training for Costa Rica police forces.

1984   Costa Rica seeks increase in military aid.

United Brands sells its banana lands but retains palm oil investments.

May   PLN organized demonstration of 30,000 people to support neutrality with the slogan "No to Armaments for Costa Rica."

Bomb explodes during press conference of contra leader Edén Pastora in La Penca with over a dozen casualties among Costa Rican and foreign journalists.

Formation of the environmentalist PEC.

June   Monge reaffirms Costa Rica's neutrality in U.S.-Nicaragua conflict, but U.S. opposition leads to resignation of foreign minister.

July   Ten-week strike by banana workers begins.

Aug.   Cabinet reshuffle, rightwing shift in government.

Agreement with USIA initiates Voice of America broadcasts in northern Costa Rica.

Sept.   IMF agreement.

Nicaragua agrees to sign Contadora treaty, but Costa Rica, El Salvador, and Honduras refuse to sign.

1985   Arrival of U.S. military training team.

1986   Formation of the Permanent Worker Council (CPT)

Feb.   Arias Sánchez of the PLN elected.

Arrival of U.S. military engineers for "Operation Peace Bridge."

June   Third revised Contadora treaty presented, Costa Rica, El Salvador, and Honduras refuse to sign.

1987

Feb.   Arias takes leadership role in regional peace initiatives, meets with representatives from El Salvador, Guatemala and Honduras in Esquipulas, Guatemala.

Aug.   Presidents of Costa Rica, El Salvador, Guatemala, Honduras, and Nicaragua sign Esquipulas II Peace Accords.

Oct.   Arias is awarded the Nobel Prize for Peace.

Nov.   Esquipulas peace accords go into effect. Costa Rica already meets most terms of compliance except for ratification of the Central American Parliament.

1988   Over half of the 170 Peace Corps volunteers in the country sign petition objecting to proposed increase to 225 volunteers as being politically motivated.

Intense debate in the legislature and the media about the formation of the Central American Parliament and Costa Rica's participation in it continue through 1988 and mid-1989.

Jan.   Continued Esquipulas peace talks in San José.

Mar.   Arias accuses countries of El Salvador, Guatemala, Honduras, and Nicaragua with not complying fully with the Esquipulas peace accords, and criticizes the presence of U.S. troops in Honduras.

Apr. After a special request brought from the White House by Morris Busby, Arias approves use of Costa Rican territory to channel humanitarian aid to the contras.

Arias travels to Washington, meets with President Bush, and requests more aid.

Arias awarded Inter-American Leadership prize by the Pan American Development Fund.

The five Central American vice-presidents meet in San José to discuss the Central American Parliament and agree to present a regional economic cooperation plan to the United Nations.

Guatemala accuses Costa Rica of noncompliance with the Esquipulas peace accords because it has failed to ratify the treaty to create the Central American Parliament.

Aug. U.S. special envoy Morris Busby comes to Costa Rica three times in one month, twice in the company of Secretary of State George Shultz.

Peace talks postponed twice.

Oct. Government condemns the incursion of Panamanian troops into Costa Rican territory.

Arias asks Contadora group to back the Esquipulas peace accords.

Nov. Agreements with Nicaragua for joint patrol of common border.

1989

Jan. Arias meets with U.S. ambassador, requests peace talks be postponed to February.

The former Minister of Public Security is accused of being a collaborator of the illegal activities of the National Security Council and Oliver North.

John Hull, U.S. citizen and longtime resident of Costa Rica, is arrested by the Office of Judicial Investigations (OIJ) for crimes against the state.

Former president Oduber admitted receiving one million colones for his electoral campaign from a U.S. citizen linked to drug trafficking.

Feb. Eleven U.S. congressmen request that Arias intervene in the arrest and trial of Hull.

Esquipulas peace talks held in El Salvador after four postponements.

Costa Rica states that because of shipping rights and potential ecological effects, an interoceanic canal cannot be built through Nicaragua on the San Juan River without Costa Rican participation.

Arias reaffirms that the five Central American presidents were very explicit in their determination to dismantle the contras.

Apr. Arias sets off on an eight-day tour to Washington and Ottawa, Canada in an executive jet belonging to Del Monte.

Costa Rica says it will not keep the contra members unwilling to return to Nicaragua after they disband.

The other four Central American nations say they will go ahead with the Central American Parliament without Costa Rica, whose Congress has not yet ratified the plan. The Andean Parliament encourages Costa Rica to ratify it.

Allegations that Panamanian dictator Noriega donated a suitcase-full of dollars to Arias' electoral campaign.

Former president Monge denies allegations that he had accepted U.S. funding for "certain operations" in exchange for supporting the contras in Costa Rica.

May	Over the last several months, Arias accused Nicaragua of noncompliance with the peace accords. Ortega sends a formal letter stating that Arias inappropriately assumed a verification role.
	Hundreds of campesinos march in San José to protest government policies.
July	Reports surface of CIA-supported anti-Noriega guerrilla forces, composed largely of ex-contras, forming along the Panama border.
Aug.	John Hull jumps bail and leaves for Miami.
Dec.	U.S. troops invade Panama, ousting Noriega.
1990	PUSC candidate Calderón Fournier elected president.
	José Figueres dies.
1991	Costa Rica becomes 100th nation to join the General Agreement on Tariffs and Trade (GATT). Government imposes emergency measures to narrow the widening fiscal and trade deficit, while workers join with small farmers to fight the government's deepening structural adjustment program.

* Sources for the chronology include: Encyclopedia of the Third World (1987); Conflict in Central America (Longman Group Ltd, 1987); Labor Organizations in Latin America, Gerald Greenfield and Sheldon Maran, editors (Greenwood Press, 1987); and Costa Rica: Balance de la Situación (CEPAS, various issues).

Bibliography

The following periodicals are useful sources of information and analysis on Costa Rica:

Aportes, Editorial Aportes para la Educación (San José), monthly, Spanish.

Barricada Internacional, *Barricada* (Managua), biweekly, English and Spanish.

Central America Report, Inforpress Centroamericana (Guatemala), biweekly, English.

Costa Rica: Balance de la Situación, Centro de Estudios para la Acción Social (San José), monthly, Spanish.

Documentos de Análisis, Centro de Estudios para la Acción Social (San José), irregular, Spanish.

Mesoamerica, Institute for Central America Studies (San José), monthly, English.

Pensamiento Propio, Coordinadora Regional de Investigaciones Económicas y Sociales (Managua), monthly, Spanish.

Semanario Universidad, Universidad de Costa Rica (San José), weekly, Spanish.

The Tico Times (San José), weekly, English.

The following books contain valuable background on a wealth of issues important to understanding Costa Rica:

Costa Rica: Crisis y Desafíos, Edelberto Torres Rivas, et.al. (San José: Departamento Ecuménico de Investigaciones, 1987).

The Costa Rica Reader, Marc Edelman and Joanne Kenen, eds. (New York: Grove Weidenfield, 1989).

Carolyn Hall, *Costa Rica: A Geographical Interpretation in Historical Perspective* (Boulder: Westview Press, 1985).

Constantino Láscaris, *El Costarricense* (San José: EDUCA, 1985).

Andrés Opazo Bernales, *Costa Rica: La Iglesia Católica y el Orden Social* (San José: Departamento Ecuménico de Investigaciones, 1987).

Mitchell A. Seligson, *Peasants of Costa Rica and the Development of Agrarian Capitalism* (Madison: University of Wisconsin, 1980).

For More Information

Resources

Centro de Capacitación para el Desarrollo (CECADE)
Apartado 447, San Pedro Montes de Oca
San José, Costa Rica

Centro de Estudios para la Acción Social (CEPAS)
Apdo. 131-1001
San José, Costa Rica

Aportes
Apartado Postal 103-1009 Fecosa
San José, Costa Rica

Mesoamerica
Apartado Postal 300-1002
San José, Costa Rica

Peace and Justice

Departamento Ecuménico de Investigaciones (DEI)
Apartado Postal 390-2070 Sabanilla
San José, Costa Rica

Friends Peace Center
Calle 15, Avenida 6 Bis, #1336
San José, Costa Rica

Human Rights

Central American Association of the Relatives of the Detained-Disappeared
(ACAFADE)
Apartado 8188-1000
San José, Costa Rica

Comisión para la Defensa de los Derechos Humanos en Centroamérica (CODEHUCA)
Apartado Postal 189
Paseo de los Estudiantes
San José, Costa Rica

Tours

Institute for Central America Studies
Apartado Postal 300-1002
San José, Costa Rica

Current Events Contact
Apartado Postal 170-2070 Sabanilla
San José, Costa Rica

Business/Official

Coalición Costarricense de Iniciativas de Desarrollo (CINDE)
Apartado Postal 4946-1000
San José, Costa Rica

Embassy of Costa Rica
1825 Connecticut Avenue NW
Washington DC 20009

Embassy of the United States in Costa Rica
APO Miami, FL 34020

U.S. State Department
Citizen's Emergency Center/Travel Information
Main State Building
Washington DC 20520
(202) 647-5225

Country Guides

If you really want to know Central America — get the whole set!

Only $9.95 each

To Order:
Each order must include $2.50 postage
and handling for the first book, and
50¢ for each additional book.

Get the whole set and save 15%!
Buy all seven Country Guides for $64.70
(includes domestic postage and handling).

Please request a free catalogue of publications

The Resource Center
Box 4506 * Albuquerque, New Mexico * 87196

Also Available

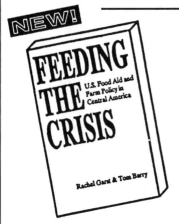

Feeding the Crisis: U.S. Food Aid and Farm Policy in Central America.
University of Nebraska Press (December 1990)

$12.95

The Soft War: The Uses and Abuses of Economic Aid in Central America (1988) studies the many U.S. government agencies involved in pacification, stabilization, nation-building, and low-intensity conflict programs in the region

$18.95

Roots of Rebellion (1987) looks behind the news flashes of earthquakes and coups to the real crisis in Central America: land and hunger

$9.00

— see reverse side for ordering information! —